CAMEL
TRAINING
MANUAL

The secret of the camel is

out...

Muslims are coming to faith in

'Isa.

Kevin Greeson

Foreword by David Garrison

Now when they had passed through Amphipolis and Apollonia, they came to Thessalonica, where there was a synagogue of the Jews. Then Paul, as his custom was, went in to them, and for three Sabbaths reasoned with them from the Scriptures.

Acts 17:1-2

Then Paul stood in the midst of the Areopagus and said, "Men of Athens, I perceive that in all things you are very religious; for as I was passing through and considering the objection of your worship, I even found an altar with this inscription: TO THE UNKNOWN GOD. Therefore, the One whom you worship without knowing, Him I proclaim to you."

Acts 17:22-23

WIGTake Resources

To order copies of the Camel Training Manual,
Phone (toll-free): (888) 795-4434 or (806) 795-4434
or Fax (toll-free): (888) 795-4471 or (806) 795-4471
or email: customerservice@lanforceinc.com

Printed at SUDHINDRA. sri_sudhindra@vsnl.com Bangalore, India
© 2004 by Kevin Greeson

Camel Training Manual

All Scripture quotations in this publication, unless otherwise indicated are from the New King James Version © Copyright 1982 Thomas Nelson, Inc.

Koran verses used in this training manual come from The Holy Qur'an, translated by M.H. Shakir, published by Tahrike Tarsile Qur'an, Inc., in 1983, AND Yusuf Ali & M. Pickthall translations as found in Alim for Windows, 1999, ISL Software Corporation.

ISBN-0-9747562-9-6

CONTENTS

Foreword

by David Garrison

If you are looking for another book about *understanding* Islam or how to *dialogue* with Muslims, then keep looking. Neither is this a book about debating or bashing Muslims. This book is about sharing the gospel with Muslims and bringing them to a saving faith in Jesus Christ. Kevin Greeson doesn't tell you how you *could* do it, he tells you how it is being done and how *you* can join in!

Greeson's *Camel Training* offers hope for a whole new relationship between Evangelical Christians and the world's hundreds of millions of Muslims. And it is a hope that is born of experience. To date, more than a quarter of a million Muslims have come to faith in Christ through the approaches described in this little book.

When I was a missionary in Egypt and North Africa a decade ago, I would have loved to have had this tool in hand. I can only imagine how God must have been at work all around me stirring the hearts of Muslim men and women. *Camel Training* provides the tools to engage those ripened souls.

Camel Training is not only for missionaries on foreign fields, though, it applies to Muslims wherever they are found, in Europe, America, or in your own community.

Christians no longer need to fear Muslims nor despise them, they can love them as God loves them and see them respond to His love in Christ as men and women from other faiths have all over the world. *Camel Training* treats Muslims with respect and invites them to confront their own sacred writings as a bridge to the good news found in the Bible.

However, evangelizing Muslims is not enough. Winning individual Muslims to Christ is not enough. Planting a church among Muslims is not enough. *Camel Training* recognizes that the world's 1.3 billion Muslims will only be reached through an explosive multiplication of indigenous churches filled with and led by Muslim-background believers, what Greeson calls *Isahi* – literally, "those belonging to Jesus."

Sound too good to be true? Then look at what God is already doing among Muslims. North Africa, Sudan, Azerbaijan, Kyrgyzstan, India, Bangladesh—God is at work across the Muslim world reaping a great harvest. The long-awaited Muslim Church Planting Movements are unfolding across the house of Islam, today!

This book and the training it offers are urgently needed by today's Christians because today is the day of salvation for Muslims. If Greeson (and the Gospel of Luke) is correct, there are thousands of "Persons of Peace" scattered throughout the world's Muslim communities just waiting for the gospel.

God is already at work in these restless seekers filling their hearts with spiritual hunger and thirst for His Word. *Camel Training* will teach you how to find these hidden friends of the Gospel and how to partner with them to stimulate Church Planting Movements across the Muslim world.

Don't wait any longer. Climb on board the CAMEL.

Preface

"I didn't know we could do that!"

"Riding the Camel is so easy."

"This is the most peaceful and effective way of witnessing to Muslims I have ever used."

These are the statements of Christians who attend the Camel Seminar. Two months after attending a Camel seminar, a new missionary flew to Karachi, Pakistan and witnessed for Jesus in three mosques. He not only walked out alive, but was invited back to share more.

Walk into any Christian bookstore and you will find numerous books on Muslim evangelism. The differences between those books and the one you have in your hand are many. Most books on Islam teach that in order to be an effective witness to Muslims you must fully understand Islam, its history and beliefs, and that the best method of winning Muslims to Christ is through a long-term friendship.

This training book is different. The Camel Training Manual teaches that:

- You can be an effective witness to Muslims regardless of how much or how little you know about Islam.

- Friendship evangelism is TOO SLOW. There are 1.3 billion Muslims in the world and they are growing faster than any other major religion. A more aggressive approach is needed.

This training book also teaches:

- That God is at work among Muslims today.
- How to find where God is at work among Muslims.
- What to say to a Muslim.
- Which Muslim to say it to.
- How to plant churches among Muslims.
- How you can be a part of a church planting movement among Muslims.

Bridges and Barriers

A bridge is designed to get us over barriers such as treacherous waterways or dangerous intersections. Once we cross a bridge, we no longer need it and can move forward. Standing in between Christians and Muslims are many barriers. So many are the points of difference, it would be exhausting to try and list each one. There are numerous bridges that can help Christians connect and communicate with Muslims. Christians wishing to effectively communicate with Muslims will use the bridges and overcome the barriers.

This training manual introduces a method for effectively communicating with Muslims. Lessons taken from a modern day indigenous church planting movement among a Muslim people group in South Asia shaped the Camel Training Manual. In this movement, over 7,000 Muslims are being baptized each month.

But why the name, "Camel Training?" The name has two meanings. First, the "Camel Method" refers to a simplified method of using the Koran as a bridge to the gospel. Numerous verses in the Koran are being used to bridge a Muslim to the truth about Jesus. The Camel Method uses a single passage in the Koran (3:42-55). For English speakers, C-A-M-E-L is an acronym used to remember the contents of this Koranic passage (**C**hosen, **A**nnouncement, **M**iracles, **E**ternal Life.)

Secondly, every Muslim knows that there are 99 names for God. Many Muslims know of an old tradition claiming that only a camel knows God's 100th name. After going through Camel Training, you too will know the secret of the camel. The Koran gives us a hint to the answer. The 100th name of God is none other than 'Isa Masi (Jesus, the Messiah).

No matter where you live in this world, you will come across Muslims. My desire is that you will be ready when you do. Without hesitation, your mouth will fall open and you will know exactly what to say. With training and a little experience, you will be ready.

Hundreds have already been trained in the Camel Method. Join us as we aggressively take the Good News to our cousins, the other Children of Abraham.

"I'll walk a mile for Camel Training!"

Acknowledgements:
Special thanks to those who have helped to explain and influence the evangelical and church planting methods presented in this training manual. These have helped to shape the Camel Method. For security reasons, full names are not used.

Koran as Bridge (Leah P.)
Experiencing God (H.B.)
Man of Peace (Thom W.)
Church Planting Movements (David G.)
T4T (Y.K.)
Discipling Muslims (Randy O.)
Seven Prophets (Scott)
Editing (Bill V., Linda S., Don, David, Sonia, Debby, Carla, Teresa, Neill)

Introduction

The first time I met Abdul[1] was in 1996 at a Muslim church planting conference where he was one of the speakers on the program. In the conference, Abdul claimed to have 20,000 baptized Muslims converts in his country. The churches in this church planting movement were considered "underground" and off limits to outsiders, especially Western missionaries.

It took me two years to earn the right to get a peek into the inner workings of this movement. My goal was to learn as much as I could and begin applying what I learned to my own church planting efforts. Riding along in a rickshaw with Abdul, he took me into four different villages that day. In each village, I interviewed the leaders of the churches and took notes. My note taking continues to this day.

That day I learned to trust my friend Abdul and see that God was indeed actively working among Muslims. I was a believer and I could not wait to take what I learned and begin applying it. I am indebted to Abdul. (Read the full story of Abdul and the church planting movement in Appendix 1.)

Of great significance for me, I learned from Abdul the method his church planters were using for evangelism. The team of church planters I was working with began using the same method. And soon, we too began to see results.

The Camel Training Manual is an attempt to package the method being used to lead more than 7,000 Muslims to faith in Christ each month in this South Asian country. The method presented in this training manual has been simplified so it will not overwhelm "beginners."

---

[1] Names have been changed throughout this document for security reasons.

Camel Training goes beyond teaching an evangelical method for reaching Muslims. Reaching Muslims for Christ is **NOT** the ultimate goal. The goal even goes beyond evangelism that results in churches. The goal of the Camel Training seminar is nothing short of training you to be a facilitator of a massive church planting movement among the Muslims in your community. Jesus' return is imminent, he's coming soon. The 1.3 billion Muslims in the world today need to hear the truth about Jesus before it is too late. We must look to methods that plunge the gospel deep into the Islamic world and then spread it like wild fire.

The Camel Trail

Our journey begins with a quick survey of what God is doing across the Muslim world. Next, we will focus our attention on the largest Muslim church planting movements in the world today.

In 1996, through Abdul, we discovered an emerging church planting movement among Muslims in the country where we lived. We will call this movement "CPM-A". Our team (comprised of foreigners and local Christians from Muslim and non-Muslim backgrounds) decided to learn all we could about how God was at work in movement CPM-A, because we wanted to see if we could apply the same principles and stimulate a *new* church planting movement. This is exactly what happened. We'll call this new church planting movement, "CPM-B."

The purpose of this training manual is to share with you the church planting movement principles that can help YOU stimulate "CPM-C" in YOUR community.

Roadblocks!

Be prepared for some roadblocks along the trail. These obstructions must be overcome or surmounted in order for you to survive the pitfalls along the trail.

The Camel trail leads you into Muslim territory. Before entering, you must be taught what to say and which Muslim to say it to. Finally, you will be given practical training for getting your new Muslim-background believer to reach out to other Muslims and form a church. But not just any church, a church that rapidly multiplies itself into a movement.

TERMS

You are entering into a world that is not your own. This world does not speak your language. To survive and thrive in the world of Islam, you must learn certain key words. Below is a brief list of vocabulary words. These terms will be used throughout this training manual. These Muslim terms may be pronounced and spelled differently depending on where you live.

Note that the word for God in this training manual is "Allah." This is controversial in some Christian circles. This issue was resolved for me when I began asking South Asian Muslims, "What is the name of the God of Abraham and creator of this world?" The unanimous answer was "Allah." Note that many of the Christian terms and Islamic terms are used interchangeably throughout the training manual. As you work your way through this manual, you will notice an increase in the use of Islamic terms.

KEY TERMS:

Allah	=	God
Imam	=	Muslim leader of a mosque or pastor of a Muslim-background church.
Injil	=	New Testament
Taurat	=	Old Testament Books of Moses
'Isa	=	Jesus
'Isahi	=	follower of Jesus
Jamat	=	Muslim-background church
Kitab	=	holy book
Masi	=	Messiah
Maryam	=	Mary, the mother of Jesus (also "Marium")
Nuh	=	Noah
Ibrahim	=	Abraham
Musa	=	Moses

Abbreviations:

CPM = Church Planting Movement

MBB = Muslim-Background Believer (baptized)
(Muslim converts prefer <u>not</u> to identity themselves with Western culture by calling themselves "Christians" instead, they prefer to identify themselves as MBBs or "'Isahi")

The Koran

Inside the Koran

This may be the first time you have looked into the Koran. Here are some helpful hints:

<u>Books in the Koran are called "Surahs."</u> Each surah has a name. Muslims typically do not refer to surahs by their number, but rather by the name of the chapter. For our study in this manual though, I provide you with the surah name and corresponding number. It's good to know both the English and Arabic names for the surahs. <u>Verses are called "Ayats."</u> Also keep in mind that as you read a variety of English Koran translations, you will quickly notice the wide range of interpretations.

Unit 1
Islam Today

In September of 1997, I laid my head down on the pillow in my hotel room in Singapore. I was attending an extended training seminar for strategy coordinators. Before slipping off into sleep, I experienced a vision from God. In that vision, I saw thousands of Muslims from the people group that I had recently adopted falling into the flames of hell. The reality of this vision impacted me to the extent that I began to cry. Tears of sorrow and fear soaked my pillow so that I had to turn the pillow over just to find a dry spot on which to lay my head.

Both the vision and the tears were unusual for me. It had been 22 years since the last time I had tears flow from my eyes. As this horrible scene was playing out in my mind, I was gripped with fear for this Muslim people group. In a few moments, the flames of hell began to diminish and a new and fresh vision came to me. In that moment, I felt the presence of God fall upon me. The Muslims that I had earlier seen falling into the flames of hell were redirected and taken up into heaven. With this peaceful assurance, I drifted off to sleep.

The next day, I became excited when I realized that at the moment I was having my vision, an estimated 30,000 Christians in the U.S.A. had awakened and were praying for my Muslim people group which was the daily focus on a widely circulated unreached people group prayer calendar. I had prayed that morning according to the prayer calendar for my people group, but forgot that as darkness was falling upon Singapore, the morning light was rising in my homeland. Mornings in the U.S.A. are prime time prayer time for most Christians.

That was a good start for a new strategy coordinator for a Muslim people group with a population of over 100 million. I knew that God was about to do something big.

The first two years were hard. Our team saw no baptisms. Our only success was that we had gathered a group of 23 Muslim women to make baskets for export. After many failed attempts to witness to these women, we decided that a new method should be used.

Meanwhile in CPM-A, the indigenous church planting movement that Abdul was leading, was seeing an explosion of baptisms and new church starts. In 1998, Abdul reported 50,000 baptisms. A church planting movement assessment team from a large mission organization conducted an extensive survey in 2002. Although they were unable to survey the entire movement, they verified a total of 90,000 baptized Muslims in one section of the movement. At the end of 2003, Abdul's central committee reported 250,000 baptized Muslims with over 8,000 churches.

Applying what we learned from CPM-A, we asked the 23 women to call their husbands for a meeting. Each brought their husbands or fathers. At the meeting, verses dealing with Jesus in the Koran were shared. From the verses in the Koran, they were shown that Jesus was more than a prophet. They displayed both excitement and anger; excitement about the truth of 'Isa and anger at Imams who had been hiding this truth. Finally, the Jesus Film in the local language was shown. What happened next was incredible.

The men insisted on meeting the next day. For four days in a row, the men met and listened as the gospel was explained to them. By the end of the week, the men were convinced that Jesus was the Son of God and the only way to heaven. They were organized into six churches.

Over the next 2 ½ years, our team saw 4,500 Muslims baptized and 314 new churches started. Nearly two years later, church planters reported that the movement had baptized a total of 15,000[2] Muslims, over 800 churches planted, and that there were no signs of slowing down.

Is God up to something?

Missionaries around the globe are excited about what they see God doing among the Muslims in their communities. Is Islam about to see a massive turning to Christ? I believe God is up to something!

According to David Garrison, "More Muslims have come to Christ in the past two decades than at any other time in history."[3] In North Africa, 16,000 Berber Muslims walked across the line and became Christians. A Turkic republic saw 4,000 Muslims come to know Jesus as Savior. A mission group in India reported that they have seen an increase from three MBBs to 1200 in only eight months. In the last decade and a half, 13,000 Kazakh Muslims came to faith in Christ.

Missiologists are not the only ones noticing that Islam's foothold in this world is slipping. Sheikh Ahmad Al Qataani; president of The Companions Lighthouse for the Science of Islamic Law in Libya, an institution specializing in graduating Imams and Islamic preachers, was recently quoted as saying on Al-Jazeera's television station, "In every hour, 667 Muslims convert to Christianity. Everyday, 16,000 Muslims convert to Christianity. Every year, 6 million Muslims convert to Christianity."[4] More than likely, the numbers that Sheikh Ahmad Al Qataani cited are too high. Nevertheless, there are those in the Islamic world who are seeing what we are seeing.

---

[2]The team reached a point where we could not give an accurate count on total baptisms and church starts. We do not have the manpower or the time to conduct such a census on the underground movement. Therefore, we resorted to giving rounded estimated numbers for baptisms and church starts.

[3] David Garrison, *Church Planting Movements* (Midlothian: WIGTake Resources, 2004), p. 99.

[4] Reported by Ali Sina, *Islam in Fast Demise*, March 31, 2004, (to see the entire transcript of the interview on Al-Jazeeras' television, go to http://www.faithfreedom.org/oped/sina31103.htm)

Join me for a look from a global perspective of what I believe is the state of the union for the Islamic world. Just as global Communism collapsed with a suddenness no one anticipated, God could be preparing Muslims for a great awakening to Christ.

SPOTLIGHT

At a theater, all eyes follow the spotlight. The one controlling the spotlight in a dark theater has control over what the audience sees. As the drama of history unfolds, the one controlling the spotlight has a beam of light fixed on the religion of Islam. Due to 9/11 and more recent events, Islam is on the world's mind. The religion that propagates itself as a religion of peace is under scrutiny. Where is this peace that Islam proclaims? Muslim leaders encouraging violence can no longer hide in the wings, they are at center stage.

The spotlight on Islam has also captured Christians' attention. Surf the Internet and you will discover numerous new websites encouraging Muslims to consider Christianity. Prayer for Muslims has escalated, especially during the time of Ramadan (Muslim 30 days of fasting). After 9/11, the largest missionary sending agency in the world quickly altered its strategic focus from a non-Islamic emphasis to a three-year world-wide Islamic emphasis.

OPEN BORDERS

Many Islamic countries, once thought to be closed to missionaries, are opening up for aggressive seed-sowing and reaping activities. Afghanistan and Iraq's borders have suddenly become easier to get through. Even countries that try to prevent missionaries from entering fail to stop the many evangelistic Internet sites and radio and television broadcasts.

ISLAM'S OWN REFORMATION

Prior to the Protestant Reformation in the year 1517, Roman Catholic priests maintained an advantage over the laymen in that they were generally the only ones who could understand the Latin Bible. Abuses became the norm as priests took advantage of their followers who could not read Latin by misinterpreting God's Word. Once the Bible was translated into the language of the people, the truth came out and the priests' misleadings were exposed. The reputations of Roman Catholic priests were questioned and massive reforms ensued. The foundation of Roman Catholicism was undermined.

Similarly, Islam today is going through its own Reformation. In 1984, King Fahd of Saudi Arabia commissioned the Koran to be translated from Arabic into every language. As long as the Koran remained in Arabic, Islamic leaders such as Imams held an enormous amount of power and control over their followers. With Muslim lay people now reading the Koran in their own languages, misinterpretations by Imams are being exposed. Key teachings from Imams, thought to be in the Koran, are in actuality not there. This has led many Muslims to question their Imams' integrity and character.

It is not only the Imams who are losing integrity. The Koran itself may be its own worst enemy. Today, some missionaries are buying Korans in the local languages and distributing them. They want Muslims to read the Koran because they know that it will likely undermine their religious foundation.

One morning in May 1999, I read a South Asian national newspaper. I was surprised to read about a member of parliament who stood before his peers and said, "What is happening to our religion? Muslims in the capital city are throwing their Korans into dumpsters, and in _____ district, they are throwing their Korans into the river."

Seeing this report in the newspaper, we began to investigate. After some time, we learned more about the events surrounding the report of Korans being thrown into the river. We discovered that one day an Imam boldly held up his Koran before the men of his mosque and said, "This book has not done anything to help us improve our lives." Then he threw it into the river. The men of the mosque, numbering 3,000-5,000 joined their leader and threw their Korans into the river as well.

ABUNDANT TOOLS

Missionaries and national Christian organizations are recognizing as never before that God has not only given Christians the mandate to go into the world and preach the gospel, but he has also provided them abundant and effective tools to get the job done. In many Muslim countries, the Koran is being used by missionaries and Muslim-background believers as the number one tool for winning Muslims to Christ. Muslim-friendly Bibles and tracts, the Jesus Film, radio ministries targeting Muslims, cassette distributions, web sites and chat rooms for Muslim seekers are among a few of the abundant tools being used today to reach Muslims for Christ. Ten to twenty years ago, many of these tools hardly existed.

INCREASING MISSIONARY FORCE

In the mid-seventies, only 2% of mission organizations around the world had missionaries working among Muslims. Today, that percentage has climbed dramatically. Between 1982 and 2001, missionaries working with Muslims have nearly doubled from an estimated 15,000 to somewhere in excess of 27,000.

B2J

"In China more than 30,000 believers are baptized everyday."[5] David Garrison describes the massive growth in China as "a church planting movement on steroids." But the CPMs in China do not see the winning of their nation as their ultimate goal. Those caught up in the China CPMs are looking beyond their borders.

Ask any church planting movement leader in China what "B2J" means, and most likely he will tell you, "2,000 years ago, the gospel originated in Jerusalem. Finally, it has reached us and now it is time to send it back to Jerusalem." In between China and Jerusalem lies the Islamic world.

---

[5] Garrison, p. 49.

The church planting movements in China have a new passion and burden for Muslims. Their goal is to establish CPMs among Muslim people groups. No group is more suited and qualified to spread the gospel into the most dangerous mission fields. Leaders in one Chinese CPM numbering 4 million members, recently told me, "The reason God has allowed us to face severe persecution in our country is only for practice...he is making us ready for the Muslim world."

DREAMS

The most revealing evidence that God's Spirit is mounting a massive movement among Muslims is the increasing number of Muslims having dreams in which Jesus appears to them. Globally, the second most prevalent means of Muslims coming to saving faith in Jesus is through dreams. A recent survey of 600 Muslims[6] who came to faith in Christ revealed that one quarter became believers as a result of a dream.

Even where missionaries are not working, God is. The most common theme in these dreams is the appearance of Jesus in a bright white robe. Some Muslims have been instructed in their dream to read about Jesus in their own Korans. Two women in Pakistan have documented their stories[7] in which it was through their dreams they were directed to follow Jesus. One of the women was instructed to read about 'Isa in her Koran. Upon reading the Koranic verses, she was compelled to find a Bible.

In the same country of CPM-A and CPM-B, a volunteer team in February 2003 decided to rent a large handmade boat and travel down a river. In the boat were 5,000 Bibles. Their intent was to distribute God's Word to remote villages along the river.

---

[6] D. Woodberry/R. Shubin, March 31, 2004. "Why I Chose Jesus," see: http://missionfrontiers.org/2001/01/muslim.htm

[7] Bilquis Sheikh, *I Dared to Call Him Father* (Grand Rapids: Baker Book House Co, date), 173 pp. and Esther Gulshan, *Torn Veil* (Great Britain,: Harper Collins, 1984), 155 pp.

One day, at the top of the river's bank, an elderly woman began yelling at the team as they were in the boat. One team member got out of the boat and approached the woman. It took a while to calm the woman down so that they could understand what she was saying.

She explained that Allah had spoken to her in a dream the night before. Allah told her that foreigners would be coming down the river that day and that they would give her Allah's book. When they placed a Bible in her hand, she raised it above her head and said, "I will take this book home and read it to my children and grand-children and then I can die in peace."

Further down the river, a Muslim man[8] (seen in the center of the picture above holding a Bible) approached the volunteer team. Like the elderly woman, he had also had a dream in which he was told to go to the river to receive Allah's book of Truth. With God's Word in hand, he disappeared into the crowd. Numerous churches have been planted along this river as a result of the volunteer team's Bible distribution trip.

---

[8] He was told in a dream to come to the river. Join the Dream Team Prayer Movement and become a prayer advocate who prays for Muslims to be visited in their dreams by the *man in the white robe*. To read more stories of dream encounters, see Appendix 2.

Unit 2

Nothing Short of a
Church Planting Movement

Time is running out for the 1.3 billion Muslims who need to hear the truth about Jesus. The fastest and most effective church planting methods for the fastest growing religion must be learned and utilized.

A new era in missions is now unfolding. We are moving into a period of time that history will record as the era of Church Planting Movements. Let's define what is meant by *Church Planting Movements*:

> A rapid and exponential increase of indigenous churches planting churches within a given people group or population segment.[9]

By breaking apart and examining existing church planting movements around the world today, you can learn what it takes to move towards a CPM in your own community. We will do this by first digging deeper into the definition of a CPM.

Consider four key words or phrases in the definition of a CPM:

Rapid – Consider the example of the television. The television was invented in the 1940's and today is found in almost every village or city on earth. To cover the entire world so quickly is rapid. In the same way, a church planting movement moves so quickly through a people group that it causes us to be amazed.

Exponential – The difference between addition and multiplication illustrates the difference between church

---

[9] David Garrison, Church Planting Movements (Richmond: International Mission Board, 1999), 160 pp.

planting and a church planting movement. One church starts two churches, those two churches start four churches, the four churches start eight churches, the eight churches start sixteen churches, and so on. As this process continues, growth becomes explosive.

Indigenous – Churches are planted within a particular culture by the people within that culture. This makes the movement indigenous. New church plants will not look like foreign Western churches. For example in a Muslim-background church, believers may sit on the floor and pray with their hands in front of them, palms facing upward.

Churches planting churches – As the movement builds momentum, the churches are no longer planted by local church planters or foreign missionaries, but by the local churches themselves. If churches are <u>not</u> being started by churches, then it is <u>not</u> a church planting movement.

Passion

Examine any church planting movement in history and you will find leaders of the movement to be people consumed with passion, passion for the lost and for church planting. They have a vision for the entire people group.

Never be satisfied with one new Muslim-background believer. Any Muslim drawing near to belief in Jesus as the one and only Savior must be viewed as the first member of the new Muslim-background church. Never be satisfied with one new MBB church. The new MBB church must be born with an instinct to reproduce and multiply itself into a movement.

To better understand the characteristics of a church planting movement, let's look closely at CPM-A located in a South Asian country.[10] After looking at CPM-A, we will examine CPM-B, the second largest Muslim CPM in the world. CPM-B

---

[10] Not all church planting movements have the same characteristics as the South Asia Muslim CPMs. To gain a more encompassing look at general characteristics of CPMs, read through Church Planting Movements by David Garrison available from www.churchplantingmovements.com

was deliberately patterned after CPM-A, but unlike CPM-A, it included vital roles for outsiders. Both CPMs hold valuable insights into how God is at work in these movements and how we can join him.

Characteristics of CPM-A

1. Identity of Evangelists and Church Planters

In CPM-A, evangelists and church planters were sent out as micro-businessmen. They earned their own salaries and most paid for their own transportation. This was done for two reasons. First, funds for salaries were not available. A small amount of funds from foreign mission sources were occasionally used to help start new businesses and for evangelists' transportation into new areas.

Secondly, funds for salaries from foreign sources were not wanted. Among Muslims in this South Asian country, non-government organizations (NGOs) earned a reputation for "buying converts" through relief and development projects for poor Muslims. Muslims have also been suspicious of NGO's for their close ties to Western Christian culture. Entering into new communities for the purpose of planting churches is easier for businessmen because they are seen as normal people with whom others can identify.

When questioned about their religion, the most common reply is, "I am an "'Isahi Muslim." They do not see the claim to be Muslim, as misleading. The Koran teaches that the followers of Jesus identified themselves as Muslims (3:53). In fact, Muslims claim that all the personalities in the Bible, beginning with Adam, are Muslims. Even Jesus was a Muslim. [The meaning of "Muslim" does not mean "follower of Mohammed." It means, "one who submits himself totally to God."] Introducing themselves as "'Isahi Muslims" always leads to conversation about the meaning of this identity which in turn gives the opportunity to witness.

2. How It Is Spreading

The gospel is typically moving along family lines. Church planting jumps beyond family lines when church planters are called out and mobilized to new frontier destinations.

3. Method of Evangelism

The Koran is used exclusively as a way of moving the conversation with a Muslim to spiritual matters. Evangelists do not limit themselves to the Camel Method in CPM-A. Since they are Muslim-background believers, they know their Korans better than outsiders. They use numerous verses which can be overwhelming for non-Muslim background evangelists.

Evangelists use the Koran to direct Muslims to see that the Bible is trustworthy. They quickly point out that in order to be a complete Muslim, one must read the "Before Books" (the OT and NT). Verses about Jesus are used to help Muslims understand that Jesus was more than a prophet. Finally, verses are cautiously used which reveal Mohammed's humanity.

Muslims coming to saving faith in Jesus retain their Korans. It is no longer read for spiritual development, but rather it becomes a tool for evangelism. This method of evangelism is a main factor for the speed by which the gospel is spreading. For evangelists using the Koran as a bridge to the gospel, they feel comfortable and more relaxed because the Koran places them on common ground with Muslims.

4. Point of Conversion

Typically, a Muslim does not receive Christ as Savior at the time of the first gospel presentation. The average time between hearing an understandable gospel presentation and actually coming to faith in Jesus Christ is three weeks to three months. It must also be noted that for most new believers, the time of conversion came when they were in the presence of an MBB. Tracts, radio programs, Bible correspondence, and dreams were tools that started them on their journey to become an MBB.

5. Baptism

Baptism follows as soon after conversion as possible. Often new believers wait until a sizable group of new believers is formed before baptism. Most baptisms are conducted in secluded locations and/or are performed at night. Almost all converts are baptized by pastors, not by evangelists or church planters. Occasionally women baptize women.

6. Terminology

Islamic terminology is used, i.e., "Jamat" is used for church and "Imam" is used for pastor. Using Christian terminology closely identifies an MBB with Western culture. Muslims are taught from an early age to reject anything that is "Christian" because Christians do not have the full truth and are sinful people.

7. The Majority of MBB's Were not Fringe Muslims

According to the study done in 2002, 66.4% of those coming to faith in Christ were active, practicing Muslims. The movement is clearly not made up of "fringe" or non-practicing Muslims. The vast majority of those converting intentionally chose to make a clean break with their past practice of Islam. According to the 2002 study, MBBs returning to Islam after baptism is extremely rare.

8. Worship and Places of Worship

Typically, *'Isa jamats* worship on Fridays. Prayer, offering, message, and singing make up the worship service. Some songs are written by new converts while most worship songs are taken from traditional Christian music. Christian terminology is changed into Islamic terminology. Out of the more than 8,000 churches that have been planted, there are only two reports of a mosque building being taken over by converts. The remaining churches meet in their villages either under a tree or on the veranda of a house.

9. Leadership Training

In CPM-A, 63% of the leaders have received and continue to receive leadership training. The CPM assessment team found no major doctrinal errors, though teaching on tithing and the ordinance of the Lord's Supper were weak. The content of the training divided its time between Bible Chronological Storying and using the Koran as an evangelistic tool.

10. Contextualized Bible

In 1997, a year before CPM-A began to take off, a contextualized Bible was introduced. A few missions had previously been circulating contextualized Muslim Bibles, but fell short of using familiar Muslim terms. For example, "Kudah" was used instead of "Allah" for God. Rarely does a Muslim use the word "Kudah" for God. When the fully contextualized Bible began to be circulated, MBBs began purchasing and distributing it with great enthusiasm. For the movement, the contextualized Bible was like a kerosene-soaked log thrown onto a fire.

11. Persecution

Persecution occurs in every instance where a Muslim becomes a follower of Jesus, but it was not as severe as anticipated. Intense persecution in the form of verbal abuse and rejection from the community typically lasts from six months to one year. Only three MBBs in this movement have been killed in which there was an apparent effort by local Muslims intent on stopping the movement. The low number of martyrs and mild persecution is credited to the technique of using the Koran as a bridge and family-based evangelism and conversions.

Characteristics of CPM-B

We learned all we could from CPM-A, and we tried to become closely involved with its day to day activities. But Abdul and his leaders knew that an outside influence, especially with Western missionaries, could critically disturb the movement. So, we knew that our job was to remain in the shadows.

But what about other areas in the country where CPM-A had not reached? We decided that we would step out of the shadows and take it upon ourselves to begin work in those areas.

As mentioned earlier, the first church, marking the beginning of CPM-B, was planted in December 1999. By May 2000, the team was seeing an average of five baptisms per week. By June 2002, we saw a total of 4,500 baptisms and 314 new churches. A survey conducted at the end of 2003 reported a total 15,000 baptisms and more than 800 churches.

Below are lessons learned and adaptations we made.

Overcame the "Outsider" Syndrome

1. Being "outsiders" was difficult at first. Quickly we made adjustments to overcome this problem. God began to send us national Christians and MBBs to join our team. Each of these men had a strong calling from God to be involved in planting churches among Muslims. Some had dreams where God called them to work with Muslims. One had quit his high paying job for a year and entered into a journey of prayer trying to figure out to what new direction God was calling him. Another bore the scars on his arms where his cousins laid electrical wires on him as a means of getting him to come back to Islam.

From 1999-2002, team membership consisted of an average of four Americans and eight national Christians. Four of the eight nationals were Christian-background and the other four were Muslim-background. These men solved the problem of the "Outsider" syndrome.

2. Security

In the beginning, the team worked under an extremely high level of security. By 1999, few results were seen. Beginning in the year 2000, security was dropped to a lower level (more open). In that same year the team began to see tremendous results. Energy spent on protection and maintaining a presence in the country was transferred to aggressive evangelism and church planting.

Living and working on the edge became the norm. Instead of avoiding local politicians, the team began approaching them and asking for permission to distribute tracts or show the Jesus Film in their area. Rarely, did a civil authority deny distribution in his area.

Other missions working among the same Muslim people group who have maintained a high level of security have seen little results. A "007" style of working secures a position on the sidelines.

3. Massive Seed-sowing

We knew that the gospel would travel along family lines. But we had no MBBs who could start the spread of the gospel to their family members. We needed a plan to solve this problem.

Since the team did not have any local churches or mission groups willing to be trained or mobilized to reach out to Muslims, the team decided to start their own Muslim-background churches. From these churches, the CPM would spread along family lines. To find Muslims who were already being called by God to become MBBs, massive seed-sowing campaigns were established.

We were not satisfied with a small scale seed-sowing campaign because we were consumed with the idea of establishing a church planting movement. The massive number of lost people demanded that we gear our efforts to be on a massive scale. Do you see the difference between the two styles of fishing in the pictures? One man is comfortable and content as he tries to catch one fish at a time. Fishing is his hobby. The fisherman using a net is hungry and uses an aggressive approach.

One of our massive seed sowing effort involved placing the contextualized Muslim-friendly Bible into every village in a particular area. This area was home to more than one million Muslims with no known MBB church. The few churches present in this area had never reached out to Muslims or had any intention of doing so. Therefore, the team joined with a volunteer team from the U.S., divided into groups of two, and traveled from village to village distributing the Bibles. The following story illustrates what they found.

One particular village encounter eventually resulted in the establishment of 41 Muslim-background churches. As our team approached the village, we were greeted by a young man walking towards us. We asked the young man, named Mamoon, to escort us into his village. The village was home to more than 7,000 Muslims. The team shared the gospel at a school and at several homes including Mamoon's.

In all, the team distributed 14 Bibles in Mamoon's village. I gave my address to Mamoon. Two weeks later, after the team had left, Mamoon showed up at my house located in the capital city. He reported to me what had occurred in his village after our team had left.

Mamoon said that three local Imams went around and collected 13 of the 14 Bibles. Before a crowd in the village, they proclaimed that the Bibles could not be trusted because Christians through the years have changed its contents. To prove their point, one Imam opened a Bible to Luke 2 and read about Joseph marrying Mary. The Bible was closed and he told the crowd, "We as Muslims know that Mary was a virgin when she gave birth to the prophet 'Isa. This Christian Bible says otherwise. It claims that Mary was married." At that, the Imams instructed some of the village children to spread the Bibles on the ground in front of the mosque. After the children danced on top of the Bibles, they gathered them into a pile and burned them.

The Imams began looking for the missing Bible. They eventually found it to be with Mamoon. Once again, a crowd was gathered, this time in front of Mamoon's house and demanded that he hand them his Bible. Mamoon refused and said, "Let me read it first, if I find any mistakes, I will give it to you." Not being satisfied, the Imams petitioned Mamoon's father to force his son to hand over the Bible. His father said, "Give my son two days, if he does not give it to you by then, you are free to do with him as you wish."

It was at that point that Mamoon found his way to my home. He wanted to be discipled because he wanted to know more about the contents of the Bible. During Mamoon's four months of discipleship, his mother wrote a letter strongly advising her son not to come back to the village because she feared that they would kill him. In the fifth month of discipleship, Mamoon was baptized. He immediately wanted to visit his village. Against the advice of his mother and myself, Mamoon traveled to his village. In his village, a large crowd gathered. He opened his Bible to Luke chapter two and explained the full story of how Mary was a virgin when she gave birth to 'Isa.

Today, a church exists in Mamoon's village. Two of the three Imams are members of this church. Mamoon has gone on to plant 14 churches and continues to plant churches to this day.

It took this massive seed-sowing effort to find where God was working. For eight days, more than 500 Bibles were distributed throughout this area, home to more than a million Muslims grouped into 400 villages. None of the other teams sent out to distribute the thousands of Bibles saw any results. But since our net was large, a single fish was discovered and as a result 14 new churches were started.

4. The Koran as a Bridge

An extra measure of boldness came to the team once they began using the Koran as a bridge to the gospel. In order to drive the conversation with a Muslim towards spiritual matters, a statement like the one below was used.

"I have discovered an amazing truth in the Koran that gives hope of eternal life in heaven. Would you read Surah Al-Imran 3:42-55 so we can talk about it?"

This opening statement, more than any other, gave the team opportunities to share the gospel with Muslims. After reading the Koran together, no Muslim could honestly say that Jesus was *only* a prophet. Our goal was to lift Jesus out of "Prophet" status and up to "Savior" status. The Koran helped us achieve this goal.

It was not uncommon to hear an entire group of Muslims say that Jesus was more than a prophet and that he is the one best suited to help them get to heaven. *Finally, we knew what to say!*

5. Contextualization

At first, the Christian-background team members felt the need to throw away their Christian identity and take on as much as they could of a Muslim identity (contextualization). Their goal was to become in appearance and practice as a traditional "Muslim" by changing their names to Muslim names, wearing Muslim clothes, and worshiping in ways similar to Muslims.

Eventually, however, contextualization became a minor issue. Muslims coming to faith actually had a distaste for Islam and were not satisfied with it. One church planter put it this way, "As we were trying to become more like them (Muslims), they (Muslims responding to the gospel) were trying to become more like us (Christians)." Those responding to the gospel did not need us to be highly contextualized. Therefore, our verbal message remained contextualized, but dressing like Muslims and efforts to get deeper into the Muslim community were minimized.

Mission agencies working in this country that maintain contextualization as their goal and try to go deep into the Muslim community are not seeing significant results.

6. A Light in the Darkness

Most South Asian countries are agrarian societies. In this type of society farmers are accustomed to working all day. As darkness approaches, they begin their journey from the fields to their village homes. Arriving at home means washing, eating, and relaxing. It is at this time that listening ears are most attentive. It is the time that stories are shared.

The team, accustomed to normal working hours of 8am-5pm, began to realize that the society's listening ears were most attentive in the evenings. Since evangelism and discipleship were best received between the hours of 9pm to 2am, evangelists began to do their visitation during these hours.

7. Rejected by Local Church Bodies

From the beginning, the team sought after the support or the establishment of partnerships of existing local churches. None showed an interest in planting Muslim-background churches or in helping us. Reasons for their reluctance varied (see

"Getting Beyond the Wall," p. 43). It should be mentioned that there were individuals in these churches who showed interest in our work, but churches as a whole did not support our work. Some churches actually tried to stop us.

In the end though, the churches' rejection turned out to be a tremendous blessing. National Christian-background church planters would say to Muslim seekers, "I have been rejected by the Christian community. You are not satisfied with Islam. Let's come together and form a new group." Church planters who communicated that they were rejected by the Christian community found a warm acceptance among Muslims.

8. Boldness

National church planters faced difficulties each time they would go out to the villages. A few were thrown in jail. However, these frightening and difficult experiences often led to the best results in church planting. The following stories are examples of this.

Hossain (a Muslim-background church planter) shared some verses in the Koran about 'Isa to a group of Jamat Islam (an Islamic radical political party) youth members. They quickly dragged Hossain to their mosque and sat him down at the feet of their Imam. They told the Imam that Hossain was teaching from the Koran and preaching Christianity. Surprisingly, the Imam said, "Study with Hossain and see if what he says is true. If he says anything false, it will come out and we will know it." This scary experience for Hossain resulted in all the youth becoming believers. Today, these youth are actively sharing their new faith with their friends and family members.

Simon (a Christian background church planter) and a new MBB named Mustak shared with two young boys about 'Isa in the Koran. The two boys ran to their Imam and told him all that Simon had said. The boys wanted to know if all they heard was true. Being intimidated, the Imam organized a mob of 300-500 and pulled Simon and Mustak into the street. At that point, the police intervened and put Simon and Mustak in jail.

In the jail, Simon was placed in the VIP cell where opposition party leaders where being held (It was an election year). He shared about 'Isa from the Koran with many of the leaders. Some requested Simon to come to their home and share all that he was telling them to their families once they were released from jail. One became a believer.

Upon Simon and Mustak's release, they both came forth from the jail praising God. Mustak, being a new believer, identified with the New Testament model of persecution and emerged from prison with his arms in the air, shouting, "I am Paul! I am Paul!"

At the trial, Simon stood before a packed courtroom. He was asked by the magistrate to share his story. Like Stephen in Acts, he boldly told the court that 'Isa, as presented in the Koran, was more than a prophet. Fearing that the courtroom could erupt into a riot, the magistrate called for a recess until the following evening.

The next morning before the trial, the magistrate came to Simon's room and said to him, "After this trial is over, I insist that you come to my house and share with my entire family what you said in the courtroom." Charges against Simon were dropped. Later, Simon shared the gospel to the magistrate's family.

Just like a contagious disease, acts of boldness by both national and international team members affected each other. As the Apostle Paul used his citizenship to get him in and out of situations, so too the international team members used their foreign status to work boldly in places the national team members were hesitant to work. As well, boldness of the national team members affected the international team members. When two of the international team members received a threatening letter which stated that if the evangelistic activities did not stop that their children would be kidnapped, the two international team members did not give a single thought about giving in to the demands of the threatening letter.

Four "OUT-Standing" CPM Principles

Let's extract four key principles learned from our study of CPM-A and CPM-B. When sharing the Camel Training Seminar with Christian groups, these four principles should be mentioned.

Speak out

When I talk to someone who does not speak my language, I must have a translator or he will simply not understand me. So we must speak to Muslims in terms that they understand and can relate to. If I use the term "Christian" to a Muslim he does not hear me say "a follower of Jesus." But rather, his thoughts go through his cultural filters and he hears me say "someone from a Western culture" who is ungodly, immoral, and does not have the final revelation from Allah! But if I use the term "'Isahi" (follower of 'Isa), I have created an opportunity to explain what someone who believes in Jesus is like without having to overcome the cultural barriers of the term "Christian." Try to use terms that they can relate to.

As a group, make a list of Christian terms that should be changed into Muslim terms.

Act out

The apostle Paul said, "..and to the Jews I became as a Jew...." (I Corithians 9:20). Where it did not violate his conscience or affect the truth of the gospel, Paul simply conformed his behavior to the people around him. To use a modern term, he became "culturally appropriate" wherever he could in order to be able to communicate the truth of the gospel. For example, when Muslims pray, they lift their hands in front of them with their palms  facing upward. If a Christian prays in this manner before eating a meal, it helps bring Muslims and Christians closer together.

What are some other actions you might adapt so the Muslims in your area will feel more comfortable with your presence?

Keep out

Do not bring new Muslim-background believers into existing traditional churches. It is not that we do not want MBBs to be around other Christians, but when we pull them into a traditional church we pull them out of their cultural setting and often cause them to be rejected by their family and friends. It is among these very family and friends that a CPM has the best opportunity to start. We should rather plant new culturally-friendly jamats within the Muslim community.

Also, unfortunately, there are those in traditional churches who do not want to see Muslims come to Christ, for various reasons (fear, loss of influence, cultural differences, etc.), thus making a large harvest among Muslims virtually impossible.

Send out

There is an old proverb that states, *"As the root goes, so goes the tree."* If the first MBBs that come to faith in Christ are trained to go out and take the gospel to their family and friends, then they will train the ones they reach to go out and take the gospel to their family and friends. Thus, churches will be planted that naturally think that they should plant other new churches. So, the pattern is established in that very first generation of believers.

A common complaint among Christians involved in Muslim church planting is that new MBBs are sent out too quickly. Keep these Christians at a distance because they will stifle the CPM. Maintain your strategy for discipling new MBBs, but do it on the run like Jesus did with his disciples. At the time when Jesus left his disciples, it would be hard for anyone to believe that these men who abandoned their leader would later change the world...but they did!

Unit 3

Bring on the CPM!

I want to be a part of a CPM among Muslims in my community, but how and where do I begin?

Good News! *You do not have to come up with a CPM strategy. God has already developed and begun work on his perfect masterplan strategy for a CPM for the Muslims in your area.* All you need to do is to find out where he is already working and join him.

At age 30, Jesus set his sights on joining God's existing CPM strategy for the people in his area. Just like you, he wanted to know where God was already working so that he could join him. The way in which Jesus went about doing this is found in John 5:17, 19-20.

"¹⁷But Jesus answered them, "My Father has been working until now, and I have been working."

¹⁹Then Jesus answered and said to them, "Most assuredly, I say to you, the Son can do nothing of Himself, but what He sees the Father do; for whatever He does, the Son also does in like manner. ²⁰For the Father loves the Son, and shows Him all things that He Himself does; and He will show Him greater works than these, that you may marvel."

Let's personalize these three verses. Write your name in the six blanks below. Read the verses out loud to yourself.

" _____ answered them, "My Father has been working until now, and _____ has been working."

...Most assuredly, I say to you, _____ can do nothing of himself, but what _____ sees the Father do; for whatever he does, _____ also does in like manner. ...and He will show _____ greater works than these, that he may marvel."

Principles on how Jesus pursued God's CPM Masterplan:

• Jesus knew God the Father was at work.

• Jesus was committed to joining the Father wherever he was working.

• Jesus knew that apart from the Father he could do nothing.

• Jesus was attentive with his spiritual eyes and ears to know where the Father was working.

• When Jesus saw where the Father was at work, he stopped what he was doing and joined him.

• The Father showed Jesus where he himself was working because he loved Jesus and wanted to give him first hand encounters with him that would amaze him and us.

1. Jesus <u>knew</u> God the Father <u>was at work.</u>
"My Father has been working until now,"

Sin came into the world separating man from God. Since that time, God has been working to restore man to himself. He has been seeking those who are lost. So you can know that God is already at work among the Muslims in your area, here are some of the works that God is possibly doing right now as you are sitting here reading this (use your imagination):

• A Muslim is feeling an overwhelming sense of hopelessness. God's Spirit is now at work in him/her preparing him/her to hear the message you are going to give him.

• Last night a Muslim had a dream where Jesus appeared to him/her and was told to search for truth. Today, he/she is looking for someone to deliver this truth to him/her.

- A gospel tract was thrown down onto the ground by an angry Muslim. Another Muslim picked it up and began reading it. As he/she began reading it, his/her heart began to burn. Now he/she wants to discuss this burning feeling with someone like you.

Whatever work God is doing, you can be assured that it is BIG. As I read through the Bible, I have not found anything small that God did. The work God desires to do among the Muslims in your area is God-sized. It is so big that we can say that it looks like a 1,000-acre field of corn that is ready to be picked ("The harvest truly is great..." Luke 10:2).

2. Jesus was committed to joining the Father wherever he was working.
"...and I have been working."

Jesus explained that he had come into the world to join the Father in the work of seeking and saving the lost. "...for the Son of Man has come to seek and to save that which was lost." (Luke 19:10) Jesus was always working together with the Father.

Have you ever been in a church planning meeting in which plans were discussed, agreed upon, and then written down. Finally, someone says, "Let's commit these plans to the Lord and ask him to bless them." Such a meeting illustrates how we often make *OUR* plans for evangelism and church planting, and then ask God to *JOIN US*.

Jesus knew that God already had established a perfect plan in his area. There was no need to develop a new plan. The only plan that was needed was the one to find where God was already working. This is your task as well.

3. Jesus knew that apart from the Father he could do nothing.
*"Most assuredly, I say to you,
the Son can do nothing of Himself,"*

If Jesus could not do work that resulted in a church planting movement, we certainly cannot either. If you develop a strategy for establishing a CPM, you will fail. Here are two suggestions for making plans and strategies:

- Make a strategy for finding where God is at work.

- Once you find where God is at work, make a new strategy on how you will join God where he is already working.

4. Jesus was attentive with his <u>spiritual eyes</u> and <u>ears</u> to know where the Father was working.

Use your spiritual eyes to see where God is at work!
In Ephesians 1:18, Paul prayed that we would be able to see, not just with our physical eyes, but with our spiritual eyes. If you look with spiritual eyes you will see where God is at work.

Read II Kings 6:14-17. What difference did it make to Elisha's servant when he saw with spiritual eyes?

Do you see what the Father is doing where you are living and working? Can Jesus help us in our efforts to see where God is at work? Let's consider the following stories about Jesus' ministry.

EXAMPLES

- **Zaccheus** – In Luke 19:1-9, Jesus came into Jericho where he was surrounded by a large crowd. The tax collector Zaccheus could not see Jesus, so he did something unusual and climbed a tree. Jesus, seeing him, sensed this was where the Father was at work, so he joined God by leaving the crowd and going to Zaccheus' house.

- **The woman at the well** – In John 4:1-42, Jesus and the disciples were on their way to Galilee. They took a shortcut through Samaria. Beside a well, he talked to a woman who came to believe that he was the Messiah. Jesus delayed his trip to Galilee and stayed in Samaria, where the Father was working.

Use your spiritual ears to find where God is at work!
"My sheep listen to my voice; I know them, and they follow me." (John 10:27)

"He who is of God hears God's words; therefore you do not hear, because you are not of God." (John 8:47)

It is very important that we hear God's voice. From these two verses we see that only the true followers of Jesus hear God when he speaks.

With your spiritual ears, you can hear where God is at work. Perhaps you have heard a Muslim say:

- "I am ashamed for the way we Muslims have been acting." (John 16:8-11)

- "I had a dream in which a prophet spoke to me." (Acts 10:30-33)

- "I want to know what the truth is." (John 16:13, 17:17)

- "I understand what the Bible is saying." (Matthew 13:10-11)

- "I think that Allah is speaking to me." (John 10:26-27)

- "I want to hear more about Isa." (John 6:44)

- "What will happen to me when I die?" (Hebrews 2:15)

If you hear someone say words like these, your spiritual ears should tell you that God is at work inside that person. The Bible tells us that only God can do these things.

5. When Jesus saw where the Father was at work, he stopped what he was doing and <u>joined</u> the Father.

"...for whatever He does, the Son also does in like manner."

When God shows you where he is at work it is his invitation for you to join him. The invitation is not for a later time, it is right then. If you recognize where God is at work and immediately check your calendar to see if you are free, you will miss God's invitation. Train yourself to respond quickly to God's invitations. When you do join him, you will see the hand of God at work and will be amazed.

- In Luke 8:41-56, we read that the daughter of Jairus was dying. Jairus came to get Jesus to come and heal his daughter. I'm sure that Jairus had one thing on his mind, "Quickly get Jesus to my daughter." On the way though, there was an interruption (or was it an invitation?) when a woman who had been suffering from a flow of blood for years touched Jesus' clothing and was healed. Even though Jairus' daughter was at the point of death, Jesus stopped to spend time with the woman because he sensed this was where the Father was working.

- Abdul, an MBB, was riding on a bus one day. He shared the gospel with a young Muslim man sitting next to him. The young man invited Abdul to come to his home right then and share the gospel with the Muslims of his village. Abdul was on his way home from a long and hard journey. To go with this young man would be out of the way, nevertheless, sensing that God was at work, Abdul accepted the invitation. As night fell on the village and lanterns were lit, Abdul continued to share with the people. At one point, a man interrupted Abdul and asked, "I have killed a man, can 'Isa forgive me?" This caused a chain reaction. Another man interrupted and asked, "I am a thief, can 'Isa forgive me?" An outbreak of confessions broke out. In the end, eleven men came forward, confessed their sins, and asked if 'Isa could forgive them. Salvation visited the village that night.

When you see and hear God at work, stop what you are doing and join him.

6. The Father <u>shows us</u> where he himself is working because he loves us and wants to give us first hand encounters with him that will amaze us.

"For the Father loves the Son and shows him all he does. Yes, to your amazement he will show him even greater things than these."

Amos 3:7 says, "Surely the Lord GOD does nothing, unless He reveals His secret to His servants the prophets."

God does not need us to execute his CPM strategy. But, because of his love for us, he invites us to join him. He knows that when we find where God is at work, we will find God himself. Our encounters with God will change us forever and will enhance our worship of him.

Second-hand God

If you ask me to introduce my children to you, I will be able to tell you exactly who they are because I see them each day. But if you ask me detailed questions about the president of the United States, I will rely on what others say about him because I do not know him personally.

If your grandchildren ask you who God is, will you tell them what you have read or what others have told you about God or will you be able to tell them who God is from your own personal encounters and experiences with him?

God is inviting you right now to join him in his new work of turning Muslims in your area to faith in Christ. By joining God in the work he is doing, you will have personal encounters with him. These encounters will truly amaze you. When asked to tell others who God is, you will share **your** stories.

Unit 4

The *Person of Peace*

In 1995, I heard a sermon from Luke 10 about "Finding the *Person of Peace.*" Five years later, I decided that I would actually try to find a *Person of Peace* (the one whom God is working inside is the *Person of Peace*) by following as closely as I could the instructions Jesus gave his disciples in Luke 10. Two friends joined me on this journey. We decided that we would take nothing with us except one change of clothes, a Bible, a Jesus Film video, and a small amount of money. We charted out a city that would be our destination. No MBB churches had been planted in that city or its surrounding area.

As we were dropped off on the side of the road to begin our journey, immediately a crowd gathered. We spent time sharing the gospel with them. Throughout the day, we continued to share the gospel with Muslims instead of going straight to our city of destination.

By the end of the day, we arrived into the city and felt discouraged because no one responded to the gospel along the road. According to Jesus' instructions, we were supposed to find a *Person of Peace* who would provide us with food and shelter. After some searching, we finally found a government office which had a small guest room attached to the back of the building and stayed there.

Just as we bedded down, we heard a knock on our door. As I opened the door, there were two Muslim men standing there. They told us that they had heard from people in the city that three men had come preaching Christianity. They had heard that I could speak their language and that I was using Muslim-friendly words. They then told us their story.

One of the two men said that a few years earlier, four foreign missionaries had come to their city and ended up going to his house. There the four men prayed over his daughter who had a problem with her leg. They prayed in the name of 'Isa. Within a few weeks, the daughter was healed and the two Muslim men were convinced of the power of 'Isa.

As these two Muslim men stood in our doorway, they explained that they needed more information about 'Isa. They understood about his healing power, but for four years they have been waiting to hear more about him. We asked the two men why the four missionaries did not tell them any more about 'Isa. They replied, "They could not speak our language." We then asked, "Why did you not go to the Christian community?" (A few miles away was a Christian community). They said that they do not like to talk to Christians. At that point I realized that using Muslim-friendly terms had separated me from the traditional Christian community.

At that moment, our spiritual radars picked up spiritual activity. With this realization, we spent the next two hours explaining how God brought salvation to people through 'Isa. We concluded in prayer.

Before they left, we asked if they could arrange a meeting in which we could share 'Isa's story with some Muslim women. We knew that if Muslim women would become believers, then the entire family would follow. Gaining access to Muslim women in order to share the gospel had been an impossible task up until that point.

Early the next morning, we found that the two men had arranged the meeting which we had requested. We were led to a village home. As we entered, we were amazed to see 25 Muslim women sitting on the floor waiting for us. For three hours, we shared the gospel with them.

When it came time to tell the story about the birth of 'Isa, we told the two men that we wanted to show a film (the Jesus Film). They quickly went into the city and returned with a rented television and video player. After the women saw the

Jesus Film, the two men fed everyone lunch. The only expense we incurred that day was the cost of a rickshaw ride to and from the meeting place. Having fully explained the gospel, we left. A church planter was immediately notified.

Six months later, we asked another national church planter to travel to the city and visit the two men. To his amazement, he discovered that 125 Muslims had been baptized and five new churches had been formed. Two years later the number of baptisms rose to 300 and there were 15 churches.

Finding a *Person of Peace*

Jesus is our model for finding where God is at work. He took the time to teach his disciples how he would do this. Jesus' encounter with Zaccheus was an example for the disciples to understand how Jesus found the person who God was working in at the time. Luke chapter 10 tells the story of the disciples' on-the-job training where they were sent out into the surrounding areas with the assignment to find the *Person of Peace*.

Read Luke 10:1-20:

[1]After these things the Lord appointed seventy others also, and sent them two by two before His face into every city and place where He Himself was about to go. [2]Then He said to them, "The harvest truly is great, but the laborers are few; therefore pray the Lord of the harvest to send out laborers into His harvest. [3]Go your way; behold, I send you out as lambs among wolves. [4]Carry neither money bag, knapsack, nor sandals; and greet no one along the road. [5]But whatever house you enter, first say, 'Peace to this house.' [6]And if a son of peace is there, your peace will rest on it; if not, it will return to you. [7]And remain in the same house, eating and drinking such things as they give, for the laborer is worthy of his wages. Do not go from house to house. [8]Whatever city you enter, and they receive you, eat such things as are set before you. [9]And heal the sick there, and say to them, "The kingdom of God has come near to you.' [10]But whatever city you enter, and they do not

receive you, go out into its streets and say, [11]"The very dust of your city which clings to us we wipe off against you. Nevertheless know this, that the kingdom of God has come near you.' [12]But I say to you that it will be more tolerable in that Day for Sodom than for that city. [13] "Woe to you, Chorazin! Woe to you, Bethsaida! For if the mighty works which were done in you had been done in Tyre and Sidon, they would have repented long ago, sitting in sackcloth and ashes. [14]But it will be more tolerable for Tyre and Sidon at the judgment than for you. [15]And you, Capernaum, who are exalted to heaven, will be brought down to Hades. [16]He who hears you hears Me, he who rejects you rejects Me, and he who rejects Me rejects Him who sent Me." [17] Then the seventy returned with joy, saying, "Lord, even the demons are subject to us in Your name." [18]And He said to them, "I saw Satan fall like lightning from heaven. [19]Behold, I give you the authority to trample on serpents and scorpions, and over all the power of the enemy, and nothing shall by any means hurt you. [20]Nevertheless do not rejoice in this, that the spirits are subject to you, but rather rejoice because your names are written in heaven."

Jesus' Instructions for Finding the *Person of Peace*

Let's examine closely Luke 10:1-20 and make notes on each aspect of the assignment Jesus gave them. Add your thoughts to my notes. Thoroughly discuss each of the points.

GO TWO BY TWO - 10:1

- Testimony of two is accepted in court (Deuteronomy 17:6).

- If one falls, the other can pick him up (Ecclesiastes 4:9-12).

- Persecution is more bearable with two.

BELIEVE IN THE HARVEST - 10:2

If you do not believe that God is preparing a large harvest in the area in which you are going, then you will not likely find where God is at work and you will miss the *Person of Peace*.

The Spirit of God has gone ahead of you and has prepared the *Person of Peace.*

WATCH OUT! - 10:3

No disciple sent out into the harvest field to find the *Person of Peace* should go without first counting the cost. Do not expect the world to act favorably towards you. Knowing ahead of time that you could end up with a black eye takes much of the sting out of the pain. A boxer knows ahead of time that he will pay a price. The punches are painful, but the boxer's mind has prepared his body to endure the pain. Unexpectd pain tends to hurt more than expected pain.

GO NEEDY - 10:4

By taking care of your own needs, it is likely that you will miss finding the *Person of Peace.* It is the God-given duty of the *Person of Peace* to take care of you. Let him perform his assignment that God has given him, you perform your duty of searching for him. His actions of generosity will be a confirmation to you that you have found the *Person of Peace.*

MAKE YOUR PRESENCE KNOWN - 10:5-6

The text says, "Whatever house you enter." This could mean, "Greet people, and knock on every door." Regardless, make your presence known in the area. Jesus told his disciples to proclaim to the people that the Kingdom of God was near whether they believed the message or not (vs. 9-11).

Also note that the *Person of Peace* is looking for you just as much as you are looking for him. If you walked into a dark room that is full of cockroaches and moths, and you turned on the light, the roaches would scramble for darkness to hide, while moths would come to the light. In the same way, shine the light of God in the area. *Persons of Peace* are like moths in that they will be drawn to you as you share the light of the gospel.

IDENTIFY THE *PERSON OF PEACE* - 10:6-8

• Accepts your greeting

• Feeds you and gives you shelter

(Not included in this verse, but should be mentioned...)

• Is ready to become a believer

• Often is a known sinner - examples: Zaccheus, Samaritan woman, man in the tombs

STAY – 10:7

This is a key principle. When you find the *Person of Peace*, invest time in him. Jesus went to Zaccheus' house. The text says, "Do not keep moving from house to house" (NAS). Switch from evangelism mode to discipleship.

> What do I do once I find the *person of peace*?

EAT AND HEAL – 10:8-9

Luke 10: 8-9 – Whether you like the *Person of Peace*'s food or not, eat it! Allow him to do his job and take care of you. Before leaving, pray for any sicknesses. You can also pray for his business or job, the community, or any personal problems.

SHAKE THE DUST OFF – 10:10-16

> What do I do if I do <u>not</u> find a *Person of Peace*?

God is not at work everywhere. (See Mark 6:1-6) When they reject you, it is not you they are rejecting, it is Jesus they are rejecting. Maintain the theme, "I will work only where I see the Father working."

RESULTS – 10:17-20

There is more to this than finding the *Person of Peace*. Jesus said, "I am the way... " (John 14:6a) When you find the "Way," you have found Jesus himself. When you find where God is at work, you find God. Remember, the happiest Christians are those who find where God is at work and join him (see Luke 10:17).

Find examples in the scriptures for each point that Jesus made in Luke 10:1-20. Tell how these stories illustrate the points above.

Summary

Here are the key principles from Luke 10 for seeking and finding the *Person of Peace*.

- Go in faith with one or two others in search of where God is working and look for the *Person of Peace*.

- Travel light.

- Don't waste time along the way. Depend on God's guidance. He will show you where to stop.

- Offer your peace. If it is accepted, stay there. If not, move on. Sometimes you will not find the *Person of Peace* until you walk away. He will pursue you. If your peace is not accepted, move on.

- Travel expecting to encounter Muslims who have been prepared by God in a dream to hear your witness.

- When you believe you have found the *Person of Peace*, go to his home. Stay with him. He will provide everything you need. He will open doors of opportunity for you to share with others.

- Whether you are accepted or rejected, always remember that God is with you and the kingdom of God is near.

- Recognize that your mission is to lead the *Person of Peace* to receive Christ and equip him to share the gospel with his family and friends.

Unit 5
Getting Beyond the Wall

Very few Christians and churches are involved in Muslim evangelism and church planting. The few who are involved are experiencing tremendous joy. I have not met an unhappy church planter who is seeing God at work among Muslims.

For others, conducting evangelism or church planting among Muslims is unthinkable. It's like they come up against a wall that prevents them from working with Muslims. The wall represents reasons for not working with Muslims. This is a man-made wall that must be overcome.

Let's identify the reasons why most Christians and churches are **not** involved in Muslim evangelism/church planting.

EXERCISE
(The questions below are designed to draw out specific fears, prejudices, or non-communication issues and then as a group take these matters before the Lord in prayer.)

<u>Individual Questions</u>: (write your answers on a sheet of paper)

What does your church think about Muslim evangelism?

How do <u>you</u> feel about witnessing to a Muslim?

<u>Group Questions</u>: (write answers on the board)

What makes people nervous about Muslim evangelism?

Common answers; fear, prejudice, do not know what to say and which Muslim to say it to.

If you were to lead a seminar on "Witnessing to Muslims", what would you teach to get people over their fear of witnessing to Muslims?

A Christian woman told me that the reason she does not want her church to evangelize Muslims is so that none will become believers and join her church. She does not want her daughter to marry an MBB young man. What would you say to this woman?

There are several stories in the Bible in which someone was asked to go to a people different from himself and to evangelize them. Some were obedient and had success. What are some of those stories?

- Jonah – Sent to Nineveh, but he went unwillingly and missed the blessing

- Peter saw a vision and was sent to the Gentiles

- Jesus with the Samaritan woman

- Paul went to the Gentiles and other non-Jews

How did they overcome the barriers of prejudice, fear, and not knowing what to say?

Conclusion

Beyond the wall is a harvest field. Beyond the wall is where God is at work. It is where you will find some of the happiest Christians. If you want to climb over the wall, you need to learn how to evangelize Muslims. Let's look at the most effective method being used today by Christian evangelists and church planters working among Muslims

Unit 6
Using the Koran as a Bridge

UDDIN'S STORY

Uddin is an educated farmer in a South Asian country. He is considered a devout Muslim because he prays five times a day and reads the Koran in Arabic. Uddin believes that Arabic is God's language.

In 2001, an MBB church planter walked into Uddin's village. Uddin quickly detected that this stranger was a Christian. Uddin asked him, "Are you preaching Christianity?" The MBB answered, "No, I am speaking what Mohammed said." At that the MBB opened a Koran and read Surah Jonah 10:94 which states, "And if you (Mohammed) are in doubt concerning that which We reveal unto you, then question those who read the Scripture (the Bible) that was before you. Verily the Truth from my Lord hath come unto thee. So be not thou of the waverers." He then read Surah The Table Spread 5:82-83 which claims that Christians are humble, friendly, and compassionate people and they know the Truth when they hear it.

Total silence fell upon Uddin, and for a time he pondered on these verses. He never had seen these verses before even though he was a student of the Koran. Finally, he looked up and said, "I want to hear another word from you."

The MBB went further to explain to Uddin that in order to be a proper Muslim (one who totally surrenders himself to God), he must read the holy books that came before the Koran (see Surah The Woman 4:136) and that he should not have any fear that God's holy Word can be changed by any man (see Surah The Cattle 6:115).

The MBB asked Uddin a convicting question, "How do we find out about the previous way of doing proper prayer, proper sacrifice, and proper fasting?" Uddin's faith was shaken. He knew that Muslims today are practicing their memorized prayers and animal sacrifices with empty hearts. He knew that Muslims are gaining weight during the month of fasting called Ramadan.

Uddin said, "We Muslims have been in the wrong way because we do not read the 'Before Books.'" He concluded by saying, "I believe your words because you have spoken to me from the Koran; please come again." The MBB gave Uddin a Bible and promised to come again. The Apostle Paul used a similar method to gain a foothold in Athens.

Read Acts 17:22-34
    [22] Then Paul stood in the midst of the Areopagus and said, "Men of Athens, I perceive that in all things you are very religious; [23]for as I was passing through and considering the objects of your worship, I even found an altar with this inscription: TO THE UNKNOWN GOD.

Therefore, the One whom you worship without knowing, Him I proclaim to you: [24]God, who made the world and everything in it, since He is Lord of heaven and earth, does not dwell in temples made with hands. [25]Nor is He worshiped with men's hands, as though He needed anything, since He gives to all life, breath, and all things. [26]And He has made from one blood every nation of men to dwell on all the face of the earth, and has determined their preappointed times and the boundaries of their dwellings, [27]so that they should seek the Lord, in the hope that they might grope for Him and find Him, though He is not far from each one of us; [28]for in Him we live and move and have our being, as also some of your own poets have said, "For we are also His offspring.' [29]Therefore, since we are the offspring of God, we ought not to think that the Divine Nature is like gold or silver or stone, something shaped by art and man's devising. [30]Truly, these times of ignorance God overlooked, but now commands all men everywhere to repent, [31]because He has appointed a day on which He will judge the world in righteousness by the Man whom He has ordained. He has given assurance of this to all by raising Him from the dead."

[32]And when they heard of the resurrection of the dead, some mocked, while others said, "We will hear you again on this matter." [33]So Paul departed from among them. [34]However, some men joined him and believed, among them Dionysius the Areopagite, a woman named Damaris, and others with them.

Questions:
- What bridges did Paul use to begin to communicate the gospel with the men of Athens? vv 23 and 28

- How does that compare with how the church planter began to communicate with Uddin by using the Koran?

- What did Paul do after he had used the bridges? vv 30-31

- What was the result? v 32

- Were *Persons of Peace* discovered? v 33

Should We Use the Koran?
Question: Is using the Koran as a bridge an acceptable means for Christians since we believe that only the Bible is the true Word of God?

Answer: There is a great divide, or chasm, between Muslims and Christians. Good Muslims have been taught from childhood that the Koran is the only true word of God. They may not know the meaning of the Koran's text, but nonetheless, they believe it is true. When approached with the Bible, Muslims immediately become defensive. A confrontation is imminent - your holy book versus his holy book. A Muslim cannot and will not deny the Koran. Relating to a Muslim from the Koran guarantees a listening ear. If attention is given to the verses in the Koran that deal with truths about Jesus, then you and your new Muslim friend can enter into dialogue on neutral ground.

Is truth any less true if it is found somewhere other than the Bible? When the Koran says that Jesus was born of a virgin without an earthly father, is it any less true than when the Bible says the same thing?

A $100 note placed between two counterfeit $100 notes does not make the genuine $100 less valuable, so long as it is known which one was real. Muslims need help in distinguishing truth surrounded by errors. You must start where they are and bring them along.

Why do we use the Koran as a bridge to the gospel?

Answer:

1) We must start where they are.

2) Using the Koran enables a Muslim-background believer to relate to his family and friends and minimizes persecution.

3) We can use the Koran to lift Jesus out of Prophet status and closer to Savior status in the mind of a Muslim.

4) Using the Koran as a bridge allows you go deep into Muslim communities.

The Camel Method is a form of using the Koran as a bridge. The Camel Method uses only one passage from the Koran – Surah Al-Imran 3:42-55.

Why do we avoid spending too much time in the Koran?

1) Though we are familiar with the Bible, and can use many different verses, we are not so familiar with the Koran.

2) It saves us from accusations of abusing or misusing the Koran.

3) When we are witnessing to a Muslim, we may be nervous and not remember all of the verses.

4) We are only looking for a *Person of Peace* and only need enough spiritual meat from the Koran to draw him out. Do not stay too long in the Koran because there are anti-Christian verses.

.

Unit 7
The Camel Method

"Using Surah Al-Imran 3:42-55 from the Koran to find a Person of Peace"

Muslims have a saying that Allah has 100 names, but a man can only know 99 of them. Only a camel knows the 100th name of Allah. Of course, that is only a legend, but we want Muslims to know what the camel supposedly knows, the unknown 100th name of Allah. We want them to know that 100th name of God, the name that is above all names - *'ISA*!

THE GOAL OF THE CAMEL METHOD: It is critical that you understand the purpose and goal of the Camel Method. It is <u>not</u> to lead a Muslim to salvation in Christ. Its purpose is to draw out a *Person of Peace*. It can also assist you to build bridges between you and the Muslim community. When you find a Muslim seeking to become an MBB, set the Koran aside and pick up your Bible.

We will use Surah Al-Imran 3:42-55 in the Koran in an attempt to raise Jesus from "Prophet" status closer to "Savior" status. After reading and explaining Surah Al-Imran 3:42-55, no Muslim can honestly say that 'Isa was merely a prophet. From the text of the Koran, it is clear that 'Isa was **more than a prophet**.

Three points from Surah Al-Imran 3:42-55 that raises Jesus closer to Savior status:

1. 'Isa is holy.

2. 'Isa has power over death.

3. 'Isa knows the way to heaven.

Exercise: Look at Surah Al-Imran 3:42-55, provided for you on the next three pages. More spiritual truths than the three mentioned above rest within these verses. As you find spiritual truths and significant observations, write them in the space provided.

The Koran
Book of Al-Imran 3:42-55

42 And when the angels said: O Maryam! surely Allah has chosen you and purified you and chosen you above the women of the world.

43 O Maryam! keep to obedience to your Lord and humble yourself, and bow down with those who bow.

44 This is of the announcements relating to the unseen which We reveal to you; and you were not with them when they cast their pens (to decide) which of them should have Maryam in his charge, and you were not with them when they contended one with another.

45 When the angels said: O Maryam, surely Allah gives you good news with a Word from Him (of one) whose name is the Messiah, 'Isa son of Maryam, worthy of regard in this world and the hereafter and of those who are made near (to Allah)

46 And he shall speak to the people when in the cradle and when of old age, and (he shall be) one of the good ones.

47 She said: My Lord! when shall there be a son (born) to I me, and man has not touched me? He said: Even so, Allah creates what He pleases; when He has decreed a matter, He only says to it, Be, and it is.

48 And He will teach him the Book and the wisdom and the Taurat and the Injil.

49 And (make him) an apostle to the children of Israel: That I have come to you with a sign from your Lord, that I determine for you out of dust like the form of a bird, then I breathe into it and it becomes a bird with Allah's permission and I heal the blind and the leprous, and bring the dead to life with Allah's permission and I inform you of what you should eat and what you should store in your houses; most surely there is a sign in this for you, if you are believers.

50 And a verifier of that which is before me of the Taurat and that I may allow you part of that which has been forbidden t you, and I have come to you with a sign from your Lord therefore be careful of (your duty to) Allah and obey me.

51 Surely Allah is my Lord and your Lord, therefore serve Him; this is the right path.

52 But when 'Isa perceived unbelief on their part, he said "Who will be my helpers in Allah's way?" The disciples said: We are helpers (in the way) of Allah: We believe in Allah and bear witness that we are submitting ones.

53 Our Lord! we believe in what Thou hast revealed and we follow the apostle, so write us down with those who bear witness.

54 And they planned and Allah (also) planned, and Allah is the best of planners.

55 And when Allah said: O 'Isa, I am going to terminate the period of your stay (on earth) and cause you to ascend unto Me and purify you of those who disbelieve and make those who follow you above those who disbelieve to the day of resurrection; then to Me shall be your return, so l will decide between you concerning that in which you differed.

CAMEL METHOD PRESENTATION STEP BY STEP

Opening Statements

The Camel Seminar assumes that you will enter into a mosque and try the Camel Method. Once this is accomplished, take the Camel Method to the streets. Since Muslims do not carry their Korans around with them, you must be patient as they either go get their Koran or they take you to their house.

If the Apostle Paul was a missionary to Muslims today, what would his strategy look like? Where would he do the Camel Method?

Paul's habit when entering a new area was to go directly to the synagogue and begin showing them Christ in **their** book, the Old Testament.

> **Acts 17:1-2 states,** "Now when they had passed through Amphipolis and Apollonia, they came to Thessalonica, where there was a synagogue of the Jews. Then Paul, as his custom was, went in to them, and for three Sabbaths reasoned with them from the Scriptures...."

How to Begin: After a friendly introduction, use one of the statements below to direct the conversation towards the Koran.

*"I have discovered an amazing truth **in the Koran** that gives hope of eternal life in heaven. Would you read Surah Al-Imran 3:42-55 so we can talk about it?"*

Or you can say:

"The Koran says some very interesting things about 'Isa. Could you read Surah Al-Imran 3:42-55 from your Koran so that we could talk about it?"

Or you can say:

"I speak to Christians and Muslims about peace and salvation. May I show what I have found about peace and salvation in the Koran? Could you please read Surah Al-Imran 3:42-55?"

But what if the Muslim I encounter does not have access to a Koran?

Recommendations:

1. Tell them from memory the three points from Surah Al-Imran 3:42-55 found in the Camel Method Outline. Encourage them to go home or to their mosque and read it for themselves. Leave your contact information with them.

2. Tell them that you believe in one God and that you are praying for people in this area. Say, "Can I pray for you? Do you or anyone in your family need prayer for healing? Are there problems in your community? Can I pray for your business or job to be successful?" Close your prayer by saying, "I ask these requests in the name and power of 'Isa Masi." Check back in with this person at a later time to see if there is any spiritual activity taking place in them.

Add two importnat ingredients to your presentation

The Rhetorical Question

A rhetorical question is a question in which the answer is already known by the one asking. Jesus used rhetorical questions because they are a powerful and peaceful way of drawing out correct answers from others. Jesus asked Peter, "...who do you say that I am?"[12] Jesus knew the answer to his question, but he wanted to draw the answer out through

58

Peter's own mouth so that Peter could hear himself say, "You are the Christ, the Son of the living God."[13]

Use rhetorical questions when walking a Muslim through the Camel Method. Sometimes, you may need to help them verbalize the correct answer. Or you may build onto their correct answer.

Attitude

By and large, Muslims are a proud people. The last thing they would want is for a Christian to approach them with a superior attitude wishing to teach them something about Allah and the Koran. Approach Muslims with a humble attitude and as a genuine learner. This is good news for Muslim evangelists just starting out. For the first time in your life, a good measure of ignorance makes you highly effective at something.

CAMEL METHOD EXPLAINED
(Basic level)

Start using the basic level of the Camel Method. This level does not refer to other ayats in the Koran. The basic level remains focused on the three points, 'Isa is holy; all-powerful; and knows the way to heaven.

I. 'Isa is Holy
3:45-47 Bring out the point that 'Isa holds the same quality of holiness that Allah has. Ask,

1) *"Does this ayat say that 'Isa came directly from Allah and that he did not have a father?"*

   Comment: They will most likely agree that 'Isa came directly from Allah and that he certainly did not have a father. Ask two more questions:

---

[1] Matthew 16:15

[2] Matthew 16:16

2) *"Are there any other prophets who did not have a father?"*

Comments: Adam did not have a father. Tell the story of Adam in the Garden and how he walked with Allah because when he was first created, Adam had no sin. He was holy and therefore could be in the presence of holy Allah. When he disobeyed Allah, he could no longer be in Allah's presence. Allah is 100% holy and nothing unholy can be in his presence. This means to us that if you want to go to heaven to be with Allah, you must be holy.

3) *"Why did Allah have 'Isa born without a father?"*

Comments: All of Adam's descendents struggle with sin. If a person is not in the blood line of Adam, he will be just like Adam before he sinned when he and Allah were both holy. As we all know, 'Isa lived his entire life without doing any sin. 'Isa was holy.

II. 'Isa has Power over Death

3:49 After reading the list over 'Isa's miracles, draw out the point that 'Isa is powerful and this power brings comfort to the world. We are naturally drawn to look closely at 'Isa because of the power he had over our greatest enemy, death.

Ask these two questions:

1) *"Do you think that one of people's greatest fears is death?"*

Comments: Death causes all of us to worry. Truly death is the most feared enemy of man.

2) *"Do you know of any other prophet who was given the power over death?"*

Comments: There is a touching story in the Injil that tells about a friend of 'Isa who died. Three days later, 'Isa arrived at the graveyard where his friend's body was placed in a tomb. 'Isa had them roll back the stone. He called out his friend's name and said, "Come out." To everyone's amazement, his friend came walking out of the tomb.

III. 'Isa Knows the Way to Heaven

3:55 Finally, use this ayat to help Muslims understand that 'Isa knows the way to heaven because he himself has traveled the straight path directly to Allah and is with Allah now. To get to Allah is a great desire for Muslims. Many believe that Mohammed can help them get into heaven. Most Muslims know that 'Isa is with Allah at this time. Ask these questions:

1) *"If you wanted to come to my house and you needed help in doing so, who is best suited to help you?"*

   Comments: Naturally, I am the one best capable of leading you to my house. I know the road that leads to my house. And who better to know the way to my house than me, after all it's my home.

2) *"I am a sinful person. I have done many good things in my life, but still I have Adam's blood in me. I know that I can never become holy on my own and get to be with Allah in heaven.* **Out of all the prophets, which one do you think is best capable of helping me get to heaven?"**

   Comments: If they answer, "'Isa is the one best able to help you get to heaven," get them to discuss why it is that they think he can help me. If they answer, "Mohammed is the one best able to help you get to heaven," then take them to Surah The Chambers 46:9. This ayat will show that Mohammed did not know where he or his followers would go after death. **Carefully** say, "If Mohammed did not know where he was going after his death, how can he help us?"

CAMEL METHOD EXPLAINED
(Advanced level)

As you continue to use the Camel Method, you can add the information below. The text for Surah Al-Imran is provided so that you can easily refer to it.

Ask your Muslim friend to read Surah Al –Imran 3:42-47. Then discuss with him/her what it says about 'Isa.

I. 'Isa is Holy

Key Points

Mary chosen by God to bear Jesus into the world

42 And when the angels said: O Maryam! surely Allah has chosen you and purified you and chosen you above the women of the world.

43 O Maryam! keep to obedience to your Lord and humble yourself, and bow down with those who bow.

44 This is of the announcements relating to the unseen which We reveal to you; and you were not with them when they cast their pens (to decide) which of them should have Maryam in his charge, and you were not with them when they contended one with another.

'Isa is the *Word of God*

'Isa is the *Messiah*

'Isa is near to Allah/God

45 When the angels said: O Maryam, surely Allah gives you good news with a Word from Him (of one) whose name is the Messiah, 'Isa son of Maryam, worthy of regard in this world and the hereafter and of those who are made near (to Allah)

'Isa is righteous

46 And he shall speak to the people when in the cradle and when of old age, and (he shall be) one of the good ones.

47 She said: My Lord! when shall there be a son (born) to I me, and man has not touched me? He said: Even so, Allah creates what He pleases; when He has decreed a matter, He only says to it, Be, and it is.

What to say about these verses:

3:42-43 (Hint: Don't spend much time with verses 42-44. These verses are only an introduction to verse 45.) At a dark moment in the history of the world, Allah did something exceptionally unusual. Allah spoke through an angel to a young virgin woman named Maryam. He told her that he had chosen her for an unusual role.

3:44 The Koran says the angels cast lots to see who would be given the privilege to guard and protect Maryam during the time period of this all-important assignment given by Allah.

3:45 Muslims have two particular designations for 'Isa. Ask: "Do you recognize the names, *"Isa-Kalimatullah'* and *"Isa-Ruhullah?"'* Ask, "Why do you call 'Isa by these two names?"

The answer is in <u>Al-Imran</u> 3:45.

Allah said that he would put his Word into Maryam. "Word" (Kalim) is related to the terms used for 'breath' or 'spirit' of Allah. 'Isa Ruhullah means, "Jesus the spirit of Allah". Another reference to 'Isa being a Word and spirit of Allah is found in The Women 4:171 "... speak the truth; the Messiah, 'Isa son of Maryam is only an apostle of Allah and his Word which he communicated to Maryam and a spirit from him."

So the Koran teaches us that 'Isa Kalimatullah or 'Isa Ruhullah was sent from Allah himself and placed in the form of a baby in Maryam. That means that 'Isa has come to us from heaven. Allah told Maryam to name the baby "'Isa Masi". Masi or Messiah means, "The Anointed or Promised One." The verse concludes with the claim that 'Isa would be honored by all people in this world and forever in heaven and is one of the nearest to Allah. It's easy for 'Isa to be near Allah since he is Allah's Kalimatullah and Ruhallah. We can also understand why 'Isa would be honored by all people of the world. Look at Surah Luqman 31:27, "And if all the trees on earth were pens and the Ocean (were ink) with seven Oceans behind it to add to its (supply) yet would not the Words (Kalim) of Allah be exhausted." Say, "I believe the Koran is exactly right. I cannot think of any major religion (Christianity, Islam, Hinduism, Buddhism) that does not give honor and respect to 'Isa." 'Isa is a prophet for the entire world.

3:46 Furthermore, Allah said that 'Isa would speak to the world, not only as an adult, but also from the cradle. How could 'Isa speak to the world as a baby from the cradle? Surah Maryam tells a story of Mary holding 'Isa in her arms. She lifts back the blanket and the infant 'Isa speaks to the people. But it could also refer to 'Isa's birth being a testimony to the whole world!

Allah also said that 'Isa would be righteous. Ask if 'Isa ever sinned. Most will agree with you that, indeed, 'Isa never sinned. Remind them that 'Isa never married, never killed anyone, and was poor. In many cultures, people considered to be holy have these three traits. Some Muslims may quickly realize that these three observations are in direct contrast to another well known prophet.

3:47 Maryam was shocked by the news that Allah had given. How could she have a baby? No man had ever touched her. But Allah explained to her that He could do anything He wanted. All he has to do is say "Be!" and it is so.

Remember: When Christians say that Jesus is the Son of God, Muslims do not understand this title as we understand it. They interpret the designation in a negative light. They think the "Son of God" title means that Allah had physical relations with Mary. To them, this is an evil insult to Allah.

IMPORTANT QUESTIONS:

- *Do you know of any other prophet who did not have a father?* Answer: <u>Al-Imran</u> 3:59 says that "Isa is like Adam. This is true, because both of these prophets did not have a father.

- Secondly, *"Allah does nothing by accident. Everything he does is his perfect plan. Have you ever thought about the reason why Allah decided 'Isa was to be born without a father?"* (Never will you have a Muslim give the correct answer to this question. Your goal is for the Muslim to ask you what you think the answer is.)

The answer is apparent when you realize that Adam, before he committed his sin in the garden and became evil, walked with God in the garden. Adam could walk and live with God **because he did not have any sin.** At first, Adam was righteous and holy, but once Adam committed sin by disobeying Allah, he and all of his descendants became unholy and could no longer live together with the holy God.

Someone may insist that although 'Isa did not have a father, he did have a mother and that she had the blood of Adam in her. This point is well taken. Explain to them that when a baby is in a mother, never is blood passed between the two. If blood is passed, very likely, both the mother and the child will die. Babies create their own blood as they develop in the mother's womb. 'Isa did not have Adam's blood in him.

Since Islam is a "works-based" religion, it is good to point out that Adam and Eve were banned from the Garden and from the presence of God because of **one single sin**. Explain what this means. Anyone who has committed only one sin has become unholy and cannot go to heaven and live in the presence of the holy God. Adam committed one sin and was cast out of God's presence without any hope of returning there. No matter how many good things man does, he cannot solve the problem of his unholiness. Only God can solve this problem for man.

The topic of Adam becoming a sinner and his descendents inheriting his sinful nature will arise. Use the Koranic verse below to help them understand that Adam was forever kicked out of the garden and his nature became evil, as did his descedents. Simply look at his descendents from Adam to Noah.

Surah Ta Ha 20:121 "Then they (Adam and his wife) both ate of it, so their evil inclinations became manifest to them, and they both began to cover themselves with leaves of the garden, and Adam disobeyed his Lord, so his life became evil."

When Adam was first created, he walked with Allah in the Garden. They could be together because both were holy. This is why the Koran says that 'Isa and Adam were similar. 'Isa was like Adam when Adam was holy. Then Adam sinned and could no longer stay with the holy God. The descendants of Adam who have Adam's blood in them are just like him. An apple tree only produces apples, it will never produce oranges. We long to be with Allah, but because we are unholy, we cannot get to Allah or heaven.

TRANSITION STATEMENT: Say, *"We need someone who is wise enough and powerful enough to help us. Is there a prophet who is wise enough and powerful enough to help us?"*

Then ask him/her to read Surah Al Imran 3:48-54

II. 'Isa has Power over Death

Allah taught 'Isa the book of wisdom and the other holy books.

'Isa heals the blind
'Isa heals the leper
'Isa raises the dead to life

48 And He will teach him the Book and the wisdom and the Taurat and the Injil.

49 And (make him) an apostle to the children of Israel: That I have come to you with a sign from your Lord, that I determine for you out of dust like the form of a bird, then I breathe into it and it becomes a bird with Allah's permission and I heal the blind and the leprous, and bring the dead to life with Allah's permission and I inform you of what you should eat and what you should store in your houses; most surely there is a sign in this for you, if you are believers.

50 And a verifier of that which is before me of the Taurat and that I may allow you part of that which has been forbidden t you, and I have come to you with a sign from your Lord therefore be careful of (your duty to) Allah and obey me.

51 Surely Allah is my Lord and your Lord, therefore serve Him; this is the right path.

52 But when 'Isa perceived unbelief on their part, he said "Who will be my helpers in Allah's way?" The disciples said: We are helpers (in the way) of Allah: We believe in Allah and bear witness that we are submitting ones.

53 Our Lord! we believe in what Thou hast revealed and we follow the apostle, so write us down with those who bear witness.

54 And they planned and Allah (also) planned, and Allah is the best of planners.

What to say about these verses:

3:48 In Surah Jonah 10:94 the Koran speaks about the "Before Books" or Scriptures (Kitabs): "And if thou (Mohammed) art in doubt as to what We reveal unto thee, then question those who have read the Scripture (that was) before thee. Verily the Truth from thy Lord hath come unto thee. So be not of the waverers."

Muslims know about the Scriptures (holy books or Kitabs) that were before. These scriptures to them include the Taurat (Torah), the Zabur (Psalms), Book of Wisdom (Proverbs, not normally mentioned by Muslims), and the Injil (Gospel). According to Surah Jonah 10:94, Allah tells Mohammed that if he has any doubts about Allah's words, then ask those who have read those books.

3:49 Allah demonstrated his power through 'Isa. The Koran says that the lepers were healed, the blind received their sight, and even the dead were raised to life again.

Don't let the first miracle listed in this ayat where 'Isa breathed life into the clay and it became a bird slip by without making a quick comment. Even though we do not accept this story, do like the Apostle Paul by using one of their stories to draw out a point. Direct them to the likeness and unity of 'Isa and Allah. Say, "Isn't it amazing that just as Allah made Adam out of clay and breathed life into it and it became alive, 'Isa had the same power to create life. He blew his "Ruh" (Spirit) into the clay and it came to life. This reaffirms that 'Isa is the Ruhullah of Allah.

QUESTION: *"What is our greatest enemy?"* or *"What bothers people the most?"* Answer: death!"

Take the opportunity to drive home the fact that 'Isa has power over our greatest enemy. No one overcomes death – **but 'Isa did!**

Say, "Once again, this passage in the Koran floods my soul with hope. 'Isa had the power to raise the dead to life– **POWER OVER DEATH!** This is amazing. The world has been waiting for a prophet who can demonstrate power over our greatest enemy- death!"

3:50 'Isa said that his life verified or confirmed what the prophets had spoken about him in the 'Before Kitabs (holy books).' The old prophets spoke much about "Isa Masi (the Promised One). When I read the 'Before Kitabs,' I found over three hundred prophecies about 'Isa spoken by the prophets. For example this one was written 758 years before the birth of 'Isa; it says: *"Therefore the Lord himself will give you a sign: The virgin will be with child and will give birth to a son, and will call him Immanuel."* (Isaiah 7:14) In the original language, the name 'Immanuel' means, 'God with us.'

3:51 'Isa said that the Straight Path is to worship Allah alone. Say, *"There is only one straight path to Allah. 'Isa knew about that straight path."*

3:52-53 In order to get all of the people of the world to worship Allah alone, 'Isa asked for some helpers. A small group of men (the disciples) came forward and said that they are Muslims and that they will help 'Isa. In addition, they said that they believe in Allah's message and the Messenger ('Isa) that he sent down (note that not all translations say, "that He sent down). Down from where? Obviously, 'Isa was sent down from heaven.

The followers of 'Isa are called, "Muslims". Use this opportunity to make a bridge. Say, "Isn't it amazing that the followers of 'Isa were called "Muslims?"

In closing of this section, ask your Muslim friend: *"Do you know of any other prophet who was given the power that 'Isa had?"*

Then ask him to read Surah 3:55

III. 'Isa Knows the Way to Heaven

"Terminate" in Arabic (mu-tawaffi-ka) means "to die." Other translations use the word "gather."

'Isa was raised to be with Allah.

Followers of 'Isa are made superior to those who disbelieve.

55 And when Allah said: O 'Isa, I am going to terminate the period of your stay (on earth) and cause you to ascend unto Me and purify you of those who disbelieve and make those who follow you above those who disbelieve to the day of resurrection; then to Me shall be your return, so l will decide between you concerning that in which you differed.

What to say about this verse:
3:55 Ask if your Muslim friend knows the Arabic word for "death." If he has the Arabic Koran, ask him to read verse 55. Phonetically, it would be, "Iz qa_lalla_hu ya_ 'isa_ inni **mutawaffika** wa ra_fi'uka ilayya wa mutahhiruka minal lazina kafaru_ wa ja_'ilul lazinattaba'u_ka fauqal lazina kafaru_ ila_ yaumil qiya_mah(ti), summa ilayya marji'ukum fa ahkumu bainakum fima_ kuntum fihi takhtalifu_n(a)." Ask what the Arabic word, "Mutawaffika" means (root of the word is "Tawaffa"). He should answer, "To die" or "Death." Ask, "Does ayat 55 say that Allah would cause 'Isa to die then raise him?"

Say *"It is exciting to read from the Koran that those who follow 'Isa and do his work will be lifted above all the Unbelievers in the world."* To reinforce this statement, show them Surah Al-Imran 3:33 (or an easy way to remember this ayat is "3-3-3") which states, "Surely Allah chose Adam and Nuh (Noah) and the descendants of Ibrahim and the descendants of Imran (father of Maryam) above the nations."

Say, "According to the ayats that you have just read, is it true that 'Isa came down from heaven, lived a holy life, had power over death, then left the earth and went to be with Allah, and is in heaven today?" Maybe there is hope for us to get to heaven after all. In Surah The Prophets 21:91 we read: *"And she (Maryam) guarded her chastity, so We breathed into her of Our spirit and made her and her son a sign for the nations."*

Along roadsides are signs that help us get to where we want to go. 'Isa is a sign for the entire world, according to the Koran.

CLOSING QUESTIONS:
Walk the Muslim you are talking with very carefully through the next two sets of questions.

> *If you wanted to get from here to my house, you would need someone to help you. Who would be the best choice to help you? Would you choose someone who has never been to my house before and admits that they do not know the way? Or would you say that the best person to help you get to my house from here would be me?*
>
> *I am a child of Adam. I am a sinner and I need help. There is no way I can get into heaven. But heaven is where I want to go. Out of all the prophets, which one knows the way to heaven and is there now? Which prophet is best able to help me get to heaven?*

Let the Muslim answer the questions.

At this point, you are finished with the Camel Method. Turn on your spiritual radar and see if God is at work.

Before you go out to use the Camel Method:

1. Before you go pray!
Pray in faith expecting results. Realize that God is already at work in this community and that there are already 'people of peace' who are open to the good news of his gospel.

2. Before you go remember these things:

- It's better that you **not** walk into a conversation with a copy of the Koran; you're only likely to offend Muslims. Instead, ask them to read from their Koran.

- In your encounter with Muslims, it is better to ask questions and draw the truth out of them than to preach the truth at them.

- **There is not** enough light in the Koran to bring them to salvation, but there are enough flickers of truth to draw out God's *Person of Peace* from among them.

- As long as you stay within the Koran and ask questions, they cannot blame or attack you for teaching about 'Isa. However, once you have drawn out the *Person of Peace*, you will be able to leave the Koran behind and teach the Word of God.

- *There is a Koranic passage that can serve as a bridge between Muslims and Christians. It is Surah The Table Spread 5:82-83, "...And thou wilt find the nearest of them in affection to those who believe (to be) those who say: Lo! We are Christians. That is because there are among them priests and monks, and because they are not proud. When they listen to that which hath been revealed unto the messenger, thou seest their eyes overflow with tears because of their recognition of the Truth. They say: Our Lord, we believe. Inscribe us as among the witnesses." While Mohammed's estimation of willingness of Christians to receive his message may have been overly optimistic, it does lay a foundation for positive relations upon which you can build.*

Unit 8

The BIG Question

After completing the Camel Method, the number one question that I have been asked by Muslims is, "Who do you say Mohammed is?" An answer to this question that belittles Mohammed can be detrimental. Muslims feel a strong sense of obligation to protect Mohammed's honor. Below, I have provided a suggested answer to this excitable question.

Who do you say Mohammed is?
Suggested answer: "I say Mohammed is who he said he was in the Koran. Let's look at Surah The Sandhills 46:9 to see what Mohammed said about himself."

Surah The Sandhills 46:9 *"I am nothing new among the Prophets; what will happen to me and to my followers, I do not know; I am only a plain warner."*

Take the time to point out the three 3 parts to this verse:
1.   He is not any different from the prophets before him. He said that he is <u>not</u> the greatest.

2.   He does not know where he or his followers are going (after death).

3.   He is only a warner.

If the opportunity opens up, contrast Mohammed's words with those of Jesus':

"Most assuredly, I say to you, he who believes in Me has everlasting life." (John 6:47)

"I go to prepare a place for you. And if I go to prepare a place for you I will come again and receive you unto myself that where I am there you may be also." John 14:1-7

Unit 9
Bridge from the Koran to the Bible

The Koran falls short of presenting the full gospel message. Therefore, you may need verses in the Koran that bridge your conversation to the Bible. Here are four verses from the Koran to help your Muslim friend understand that Allah's Truth and roadmap to heaven is perfectly revealed in the "Scriptures that came before the Koran." First look at Surah Jonah 10:94:

> *And if you (Mohammed) are in doubt concerning that which We reveal unto you, then question those who read **the Scripture** (that was) **before you**. Verily the Truth from thy Lord hath come unto you. So be not of the waverers.*

Allah tells Mohammed, if you have doubts, you should question *"those who read the Scripture that was before you,"* because the truth is found in those Scriptures. Christians and Jews are the ones who have read the previous scriptures referred to by Mohammed.

Then, ask your friend to read Surah The Women 4:136:

> *O you who believe! Believe in Allah and His messenger and the Scripture which He has revealed unto His messenger, and **the Scripture which He revealed aforetime**. Whosoever **disbelieves** in Allah and His angels and His **Scriptures** and His messengers and the Last day he verily has wandered far astray*

It is common for Muslims to allege that the Scriptures "that came before," that is the Old and New Testaments, have been changed and corrupted and are therefore unreliable. Refer them to Surah Cattle 6:115-116 which reads:

...Those unto whom We gave the Scripture (aforetime) know that it is revealed from your Lord in truth. So be not (O Mohammed) of the waverers. Perfected is the Word of the Lord in truth and justice. There is nothing that can change His words. He is the Hearer, the Knower.

So, Allah has assured Mohammed that the Scripture (prior to the Koran) was given by him. It is perfect and no one can change it.

Finally, show your friend that the roadmap for blessings and eternal life are found in the Taurat and Injil. Read The Table Spread 5:65-66

If only the People of the Scripture (the Jews – see verse 64) would believe and ward off evil, we would remit their sins from them and surely We would bring them into Gardens of Delight. If they had observed the **Taurat (Torah) and the Injil (Gospel)** *and that which was revealed unto them by their Lord, then they would have been nourished from above them and from beneath their feet.*

SUMMARY

Surah Jonah 10:94 – Have doubts? Go to the people who have the 'Before scripture."

Sura The Women 4:136 – Don't be a wanderer, believe in the "Before scriptures."

Surah Cattle 6:115-116 – Allah's words cannot be changed.

Surah The Table Spread 5:65-66 – Roadmap for blessings and eternal life.

Let's find a way to help us to remember these verses:

1. Remove the Surah numbers.

2. Group the first two verses together into a sentence, then the next two:

"When Jonah was 94, he warned 136 women."

"115 cattle taste best on my 65 tables"

Use the space below if you can think of an easier way to remember these verses.

Unit 10
Who to Say It to

If you help people know what to say and who to say it to, many
will attempt to try it. From this training, you acquired some
tools that you can use to reach out to Muslims. You have
learned **what to say**:

> *"I have discovered an amazing truth in the Koran*
> *that gives hope of eternal life in heaven. Would you*
> *read Surah Al-Imran 3:42-55 so we can talk about*
> *it?"*

Now let's answer the question, **who do you say it to**? Using
the Camel Method you can begin a conversation with a
Muslim or groups of Muslims almost anywhere, even in a
mosque. As you share the Camel Method, keep your spiritual
eyes and ears open. God may be working in the heart of
someone. You will determine with whom to use the Camel
Method by completing the following exercise.

1. Get a partner
Jesus sent his disciples out two by two. Together with your
partner, make an appointment to do the Camel Method with
Muslims in your community.

2. Make a list
- Make a list of 8 Muslims in your community. If you do not
  know names, simply write a description such as "butcher
  at the market" or write the name of locations in your
  community where you know Muslims reside.

- From the list of eight, choose two with whom you will share
  the Camel Method this week. Each week continue to share

with two names from the list of 8 until you find the *Person of Peace.*

Write in the blanks below the names or descriptions of 8 Muslims

1. _____

2. _____

3. _____

4. _____

5. _____

6. _____

7. _____

8. _____

2 Muslims (from list above) this week that I will share the Camel with:

1. _____

2. _____

3. Go and do it.

Don't forget to revisit Muslims who do not receive Jesus as Savior but yet show an earnest interest or invites you to come back. Muslims need time to think.

Unit 11

Illustrated Version of Camel Training

David attends a Camel Training Seminar. He learns what to say.

He makes a list of eight Muslims with whom he will share the Camel Method.

David writes the names of the 8 Muslims on his calendar.

			1	2	3	4	5
6	7 BILLAL	8	9	10 SHAH	11	12	
13	14	15 SHAHADAT	16	17	18	19 MOHAMMED	
20	21 JALAL	22	23	24 MOMEEN	25	26	
27 ALI	28	29 HOSSEIN	30	31			

He then prepares for going out to find the *Person of Peace.*

David goes out and shares the Camel Method with the eight Muslims on his list until he finds a *Person of Peace*.

Possible *Persons of Peace.*

David finds Mustafa - The *Person of Peace.*

David goes to Mustafa's house. He finishes using the Koran as a bridge.

David has Mustafa lay the Koran aside. David tells Mustafa how to become a follower of 'Isa. He visits Mustafa each day for 5 days for discipleship. (For a basic guideline for discipling a new MBB, see Appendix 4.)

David teaches Mustafa what to say (Camel Method) and who to say it to (Mustafa makes list of 8 Muslim names.)

Mustafa goes out to do the Camel Method with the 8 Muslims on his list, two each week.

David stays behind and prays for Mustafa.

Mustafa finds the *Person of Peace*

Mustafa trains the *Person of Peace* to use the Camel Method and has him make a list of 8 Muslims. Mustafa sends him out.

Mustafa gathers the MBBs and organizes a jamat.

APPENDIX 1

A Muslim Meets an Angel
(How the South Asia CPM-A Began)

Growing up in a South Asian Muslim village requires most young boys to attend a school which teaches the reading and memorization of the Koran in Arabic. This school, called a "madrassa", prepares him to be a potential Imam. For Abdul Mohammed (not his real name), life was no different, and at the age of nine he was sent to the madrassa. Abdul dedicated himself to his lessons and prayers, but as he delved deep into the Koran, he began to have many disturbing questions about its validity and meaning. The first time he questioned the authority of the Koran, he was beaten and instructed never to ask about the meaning of anything in the Koran again. Nevertheless, a bit later, he once again voiced his concern about the meaning of a particular passage in the Koran. This time he was banned from the madrassa and sent home in disgrace. A note was placed on the bulletin board of the madrassa stating, "Abdul is a sinner boy and anyone who talks to him will also be shamed."

Branded forever in shame, Abdul's father built a shack behind their house for him to live in. For three years, no one was allowed to talk to him, touch him or look at him. He lived in solitude. Not being allowed to eat with his family, his mother had to bring him his meals and slide them through a hole in the door. It didn't take long for him to decide that living without human interaction was no way to live. One day, in an attempt to kill himself, he drank poison that his father used on the farm. His mother heard his vomiting and rushed him to the hospital.

Abdul's stay in the hospital proved to be the happiest time of his childhood. There he was surrounded continually by caring people and received a lot of much needed attention. Yet, going home was inevitable. Not long after his return, he again attempted suicide.

When he turned thirteen, his time of solitude was over. However the declaration that he was a "sinner boy" still served to isolate him from society forever. People still treated him as though he was cursed, he had no friends, and people continued to avoid him.

One afternoon while Abdul was walking on a village road, a white man in a rickshaw stopped and asked if he needed a ride. The man in the rickshaw was a missionary. This was the first white man Abdul had ever seen. He stood paralyzed in shock because the white man had spoken to him. He also wondered why this man didn't care if he was seen talking with Abdul in public. While riding together on the rickshaw, Abdul touched the white man's arm to see if he was a man or an angel. They rode together to the man's home. There Abdul learned that the man was not only a Christian, but he was also the owner of several Bibles. Abdul did not even think that Bibles existed. After drinking his very first coffee, Abdul left with a New Testament in his hand.

Arriving back at his home, he opened the Bible and read the first book he came to - the Gospel of John. When he read John 3:17, he was astounded. It said that God did not condemn him. For his entire life he had been condemned by everyone, and he thought that God condemned him as well. That night, he realized that God loved him and so Abdul accepted God's grace.

From that time forward, Abdul's cursed little room on the side of his father's house became a glorious haven for him. There he could study the scripture without anyone knowing. Desiring more teaching, Abdul asked the missionary to teach him, so he arranged for a local pastor to disciple Abdul.

Soon Abdul began to attend church. When news of this eventually came to his father, he told him to stop going to the Christian church. Abdul told his father that *he would try* to stop going. Abdul jokingly states, "But when Sunday came, I tried to not go to the church, but my feet would not listen and they took me directly there."

As a result of Abdul's direct disobedience, an emergency family meeting was held with all of Abdul's uncles. They discussed Abdul's predicament. It was quickly resolved that by beating him, this evil spirit will come out of him. So they began to unmercifully beat Abdul until his favorite uncle couldn't tolerate the mistreatment anymore. He suggested another method in solving this problem. He told Abdul's father and uncles that the problem could be solved and forgotten if Abdul would renounce Jesus and burn the Bible in front of them. They all agreed.

Abdul knew that his life had been worthless before Jesus and he didn't want to give up the peace he had been given. When he refused to renounce Jesus and burn his Bible, the uncles tied Abdul to a stake in his family's courtyard in an attempt to make Abdul change his mind. Before the next sunrise, his mother quietly came to Abdul's side and untied him. She gave him the equivalent of US $5.00 and instructed him to leave before his uncles killed him. That was the last time he saw his mother alive. Later, for disgracing her husband, his mother was mistreated by Abdul's father. She was abused and beaten. As a result of this mistreatment, she died.

Abdul immediately went to the white missionary's house. The missionary put the equivalent of US $12.00 in Abdul's pocket and told him to go to his office in the capital city. As he journeyed to the capital city, his money was stolen, and he was forced to sleep on the street for 15 days. This was his first time in the capital city, and he did not know where the missionary's office was. He survived by scrounging for leftover food that was thrown into the street. He ate banana peels and whatever else he could find.

Eventually, he found the missionary's office, yet, not having a bath and looking like a beggar, the office guard would not admit him. Thankfully, as Abdul was leaving the gate, the missionary saw Abdul from his window, realized who he was, and let him in. After he was fed, cleaned up and clothed, Abdul was introduced to a local Baptist pastor who mentored him and prepared him for baptism.

At the baptismal service, the church leaders refused to allow Abdul to be baptized. They told him to first change his name, and then he would be allowed to be baptized. Abdul refused to change his name. He told the church leaders that his name was his testimony to other Muslims so that they could understand that Muslims can become Christians. Because of Abdul's courage and adamancy, the pastor yielded and baptized him anyway.

In the capital city, Abdul received a university degree and a Master's degree. Then he returned to his boyhood village, but still he was not allowed to return to his home. People in the community had heard that Abdul had become a Christian. One day while walking through an open field, a large group of boys saw Abdul and caught him. Each of the boys took turns beating him. After a while, a local politician came walking by and asked the boys why they were beating this boy. They told him, "We caught a Christian and we are going to kill him." The politician convinced the boys that they would bring trouble upon the entire community if they killed this Christian boy. They complied, but as they left, they each walked by Abdul's motionless body and spat on him.

Hearing the news of the beating, Rafik, a school classmate of Abdul's, came and took Abdul to his home. Over the course of several days, Abdul told Rafik all about his new faith in Jesus. Responding to this information, Rafik wanted to be baptized. Abdul refused to baptize Rafik because he did not want him to encounter the same persecution that he had. Rafik told Abdul that he didn't care about the persecution he would face, and that if Abdul would not baptize him, then he would think that Abdul was a hypocrite. Rafik stepped into the river and

Abdul baptized him. Abdul told Rafik, "Yesterday, I was one, today, we are two; tomorrow we could be two hundred."

Around that same time, Abdul's father became seriously ill and was on the threshold of death. He sent word for Abdul to come visit him. Eight years had passed since he had seen his father. Abdul sat beside his father's bed and openly prayed for him. The next day his father sent for Abdul again. His father was in amazement! After praying for weeks and weeks to God nothing had happened, yet when his son prayed only one time, he was quickly feeling better. He asked if Abdul would pray for him again, each day, until he was totally healed.

Eight years prior to this, Abdul's father had filed a legal document with the local court that his son Abdul was dead. Now fully recovered from his illness, his father received Jesus as his Savior and was baptized by Abdul.

A relative of Rafik was sent to talk to Rafik and Abdul about returning to Islam. But rather than convincing them, the relative's own faith was shaken. Two weeks later, word came to Rafik requesting him to travel to the village where this relative lived. Rafik journeyed to the village and remained there for several days. Upon his return, he shared with Abdul the news, "I baptized seven families (totaling 36 people) in my relative's village."

These baptisms were a great encouragement to Abdul and Rafik. They began to travel and share about the grace and miraculous love the Lord desires to give all people. They began by first reaching their own families and then slowly reaching their friends.

In May 2002, a CPM assessment team from a large mission agency conducted a survey in the area where Abdul and Rafik have been working. From the report, it was noted:

The mission agency team verified through extensive, mostly on-site, interviews, with many of a random nature, that a Church Planting Movement of historic size, scope and spiritual depth among Muslims anywhere, emerged among the (South

<u>Asian Muslim people group)</u> during the late 1990s and is continuing amidst significant and escalating persecution.

Rafik's bamboo house became the hub of the movement. Abdul estimates that Rafik ran more than 4000 Muslim converts through his discipleship program over a period of eight years. Each batch of disciples would meet in the bamboo house for a fifteen day period of time.

In February 2003, late one night, Rafik answered a knock on his door. When Rafik opened his door, a group of fundamentalist Muslims rushed in and stabbed Rafik to death. Abdul remains in the area living with his family and continues to lead the movement. But the discipleship arm of the movement has taken a severe loss.

The primary means by which this movement has progressed is that of using passages in the Koran, which speak of Jesus, as a bridge to engage Muslims in conversation about Jesus. From there, passages in the Koran that encourage Muslims to read the Bible are used to challenge Muslims to look at what the Bible says about Jesus. Completing the bridge to the Bible, Muslims are brought to faith in Jesus.

APPENDIX 2

Dreams

The most common way that Muslims are drawn to Jesus is through a direct verbal witness. The 2nd most common way that Muslims are coming to Christ is through dreams and visions. The most common image seen in these dreams is Jesus. He is usually illuminated and wearing a white robe.

Each year, thousands of Muslims across the globe are reporting that they are having dreams in which 'Isa appears to them. These dreams are causing them to re-evaluate what they previously believed about the prophet 'Isa. Some miracles are being reported as well.

Ongoing research is underway concerning reports of Muslims seeing 'Isa in their dreams. One group that is collecting written summaries of "'Isa" dreams has posted them on their website (see www.'IsaalMasi.net).

The Dream Team

You can join God in his work among Muslims through prayer. If you live in the Western hemisphere, pray in the morning time for Muslims. Your morning prayer coincidences with the time in which most Muslims are going to sleep. Pray that the man in the white illuminated robe would appear and speak to them. Start a Dream Team Prayer Movement in your church.

Dream Encounters from South Asia

Momeen

Momeen lived in a large South Asian city for 16 years as an Imam. He was saying his prayers in a large mosque where 5000 men came to pray each day. He used to preach against

Jesus and Christians. On December 25th, 1996, during the night of Shabi Barat he was asked to come and teach about the big night from 10:30 pm until 1 am. That night he spoke against Christians saying they were dancing and drinking during this holy night. Many Muslims believe that Christians are womanizers and drunks.

After teaching, Momeen went for rest, he was supposed to return at 4 a.m.—but this is when his vision or dream began. He saw two men coming to lift him, one on the left and one on the right. They took him five steps and then disappeared. He no longer saw the mosque, but he did see a big hall with a curtain. "How did I get here?" he wondered, and "Where are the two men?" Momeen saw the curtain drawn back and a magnificent light. When he saw the light he heard a loud voice say, "Come near to me, I love you very much." Surprised, he did not know who was speaking, so he asked, "Who are you?" The voice said, "I am Christ." At that moment his whole body was overjoyed and filled with excitement. Then he received a glass of water and was told to drink it, that it would change his life. He drank the water and his body felt very light. As he was doing this, the light went away.

He woke up and found himself standing in the place he had been sleeping. It was now 4 am; from 1 a.m. to 4 a.m. he had been standing throughout his vision. It was now time for the morning prayers, but he told his assistant, "You do the morning prayers at the mosque." He then went home and told his family about his vision. They were very happy for him. Still, he did not understand why he had had the vision. He was surprised that he did not know, because he was proud, thinking that he knew everything.

From that time on he could no longer pray. He gave the duty of the prayers to his assistant, always saying that he was sick and then going home. At home on a Saturday night he again had a visitation; this time he was sitting. Over the course of four months he had six visitations. In each vision, God spoke to him. On the sixth visit God said, "I have chosen you to go, read and meditate on the New Testament." He was instructed in the dream to meet with a friend who had a New Testament.

Momeen was surprised to learn that there was a Bible in Hindi. He had thought that the Bible was only in English and that only English people read it. He met with his friend who took him to the Salvation Army. There a Bishop listened to his story. The Bishop introduced him to a man who would disciple him. In 36 days he had finished reading the New Testament. Then God spoke to Momeen again and told him that he would have a voice to thousands of Muslims. "But how?" Momeen wondered. Today Momeen's visions are still with him. He now distributes a newspaper to Muslims, which shares the theme that God wants to speak to them through the Bible. He receives at least ten calls a day from Muslims inquiring about his message.

Hossain

A Muslim man in Bangladesh had a dream where he saw 'Isa standing in the middle of a large crowd. Individuals in the crowd pressed hard to get close enough to 'Isa to see his face. 'Isa's face was hidden underneath the hood of his robe. Longing to see 'Isa's face as well, he pushed his way through the crowd. He woke up just before getting to 'Isa. Over a period of four years, the man longed to see 'Isa's face. Finally, on a trip to the capital city, he walked into the foyer of a Catholic church and saw a picture of 'Isa on the wall. This brought him great satisfaction and immediately found a group of Christians who would tell him more about 'Isa.

Raja

Taken to the Madrassa at age five by his parents, Raja, was on his way to becoming an Imam. As a teenage Imam, he was consumed with pride and thought that he knew everything. One day, a Bengali Christian woman visited his Madrassa. She was allowed to briefly speak to the Madrassa students. Quickly Raja angerly shouted at her and forced her to leave.

That night, he had a disturbing dream. He dreamed that he was in his house with his family. Suddenly, the house was surrounded with people who slowly kept moving in closer to his house. The people were angry at him for running off the Christian woman. This dream disturbed him deeply. Raja said, "Still to this day, the hatred that I showed to the Christian woman visits me from time to time."

The reoccurring thoughts about this incident caused Raja to look closer into what the Christian woman taught that day at the Madrassa. She had mentioned that 'Isa was born from a virgin and that he is the only one who can guarantee salvation. Several years later, Raja wanted to become a village (homeopathic) doctor. He received training from an experienced doctor who once was a Muslim, but had become a follower of 'Isa. This doctor helped Raja study the passages in the Koran that deals with 'Isa. Raja learned and accepted that 'Isa was righteous, honorable, and knows the way to heaven. Today, Raja reads his Bible. He knows fully that 'Isa is the only way to heaven and was baptized.

As a doctor, Raja gives medicine to his patients, but never fails to pray for healing in the name of 'Isa. Raja said, "I have dedicated my life to sharing 'Isa to the world." He is now writing a book for Muslims so they can understand that 'Isa is the only way to heaven.

Raja now has better dreams, dreams that encourage and draw him to his Savior. Recently, he had a dream where he saw a huge light and then 'Isa and the twelve disciples appeared. Dreams like these only increase his desire to share the love of a loving Savior with everyone around him. When patients return to his doctor's office, he teaches them about 'Isa by using the Koran.

His boldness is infectious, as he stands up for his Lord. One evening in December 2002, he attended the mosque in which he previously was an Imam. On this particular evening, Muslims believe God sends out his heavenly angels to listen to people's petitions. Three hundred Muslim men were in attendance that night in the mosque. Raja stood up before them all and told them that 'Isa is the Savior and he began to teach from the Koran. He said, "This is the night to find salvation in 'Isa, if you are looking and want to be baptized please come with me to the pond and be baptized." Eight men stood to their feet and walked out of the mosque into the darkness and found for themselves the light that Raja had found.

Mohammed

Constantly plagued by dreams, Mohammed rarely slept well. One particular evening he had a dream that a man came and told him, "Get up." Not responding to the man's earnest plea, the man shouted at him and urgently told him not to sleep but to wakeup! For many days he continued to hear the voice telling him to get up. He was sixteen years old at this time and he had no idea what the voice meant.

Two weeks later the voice came again but this time it said, "Go preach salvation!" Mohammed didn't know what salvation was but he knew that he must obey the voice. He went to Dr. Shahim, a friend and mentor for some advice. Dr. Shahim also desired to find the correct way to heaven and thought he had found it. He quickly instructed Mohammed that there was one way to heaven and it was through a pir (Muslim holy man) in India named Khaza Moynoddin Chishty. Obviously the doctor wasn't a Christian, and although he thought he knew the truth he was gravely mistaken.

A few years later though, Dr. Shahim was presented with the truth of the gospel and he made sure to correct his wrong instruction. Mohammed immediately went to Dr. Shahim's home with some of his disciples and they discussed the Lord all evening.

When Mohammed finally understood the truth that 'Isa is the one and only Savior, he wanted to be baptized. Dr. Shahim told him that it was late and that in the morning, they will do baptism. Mohammed asked Dr. Shalim, "What would happen if something happened to me between now and in the morning...please baptize me now." Late into the night, Mohammed and four others were baptized. Mohammed began traveling from village to village sharing the story of the virgin birth of 'Isa, that 'Isa is the sinless son of God, our Rock and Redeemer, and friend.

Ali

About his childhood, Ali said that he was especially mischievous and everyone in his village labeled him as an unruly boy. Not knowing what else to do with Ali, his father sent him to the madrassa. Ali did well at the madrassa; he delved into his studies and learned the importance of being holy. His Madrassa teacher taught him the correct way to pray as a Muslim and for twelve years he was the Imam of his village mosque.

During these twelve years, he served God and strove to be faithful, but in the back of his mind, there was a nagging thought; "How can a man become truly holy." This frustrated Ali to the point that it caused him to began looking for 'good' men who could instruct him in correct teaching. Eventually, he met a Muslim friend who had become a believer.

After hearing the truth about 'Isa being the one and only Savior, Ali went home that evening pondered this truth. That night, he dreamt that a man in a white robe appeared before him and he showed Ali a village pond. Then he said, "Go there and get a bath." Still in his dream, Ali obeyed the man and went down into the water. Coming out of the water, he noticed an open cut over his heart. The man in the white robe touched him and it closed immediately. Ali awoke in a cold sweat and rushed to his believer friend's house with a desperate desire to be baptized, knowing that it was the True Way. The next afternoon while he was eating lunch, Ali saw a vision. He saw a river of blood rushing toward him and then a white cloud appeared. He realized that he was seeing the blood of Jesus that was shed for him, and then he read in the Bible that 'Isa will come back in the clouds. Ali continues to seek the truth and everyday he chooses to follow 'Isa and no other. He is the pastor of a small Muslim-background church.

APPENDIX 3
The Korbani
Plan of Salvation

Introduction

Rarely does a Muslim in the first evangelistic encounter acknowledge that he is ready to receive Christ as his Savior. When he or she does display an interest, you should be ready to tell him or her how to be saved from their sin. An excellent tool for conveying the truth that Jesus died as the sacrifice for our sins is the *Korbani Plan of Salvation*.

"Korbani" is the Islamic word for sacrifice (spelling may be different in some parts of the world). A good Muslim is 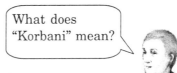 supposed to practice the act of Korbani once each year, if he can afford it, but at least once in his lifetime. This event falls not long after the month of fasting, Ramadan. It can be offered for an individual, but usually one sacrifice covers an entire family. Whether Muslims actually practice the Korbani depends on whether they can afford it or not.

When asked about the origin of the Korbani, a Muslim is quick to answer that this practice is based on Abraham's offer to sacrifice his son on the mountain. They will insist that Abraham took Ishmael to the mountain to be sacrificed. Even though this is not stated in the Koran, now is not the time to argue about this issue.

Although the practice of Korbani is deeply rooted in Islam, very few Muslims understand the reason God established the sacrificial system. When asked about the history and meaning of Korbani, most Muslims will say that they practice Korbani because their father, his father, and his father practiced this ritual.

The sacrifice can be a goat, sheep, cow, or camel. The actual sacrifice may not be the same in all parts of the world. Normally, an animal is purchased a few days before Korbani Eid (ee-d – annual ceremonial sacrifice of an animal by Muslims, similar to animal sacrificing found in the Old Testament). The animal must be in good condition.

Typically, on the morning of Korbani Eid, the family dresses in their finest clothes and gathers in the yard. The male leader of the family along with other males in the family place their hands on the animal. The leader has in his hand a written list of seven names of special family members, some who have already deceased. A prayer is said and then the names on the list are called out immediately before the animal's throat is cut. A local butcher, with a proper knife, slits the throat of the animal.

Afterwards, the family returns to the house and the butcher goes to work on dividing up the meat for distribution. It is required that a portion of the meat be given to the poor.

The Korbani Plan of Salvation should be shared with a Muslim only after the Camel method has been presented. Remember that the Korbani Plan of Salvation should only be presented to Muslims who are open to receiving the Truth.

The Korbani Plan of Salvation
Step by Step

POINT 1
Ibrahim Offered a Korbani

Ask these questions:

Do you know the story of Hazrat Ibrahim (*Hazrat* = a term of honor like "sir". Ibrahim = Abraham) and when he was told to do *Korbani* with his son?

What did Hazrat Ibrahim do? Answer: Ibrahim took his son to offer as a Korbani.

What did Allah do at the last minute? Answer: He sent an angel to stop the Korbani.

What test was Allah giving to Ibrahim? Answer: To see how much Ibrahim loved Allah.

As Ibrahim and his son walked up the mountain, what did Ibrahim's son ask him? Answer: "The fire and the wood are here, but where is the lamb for the burnt offering?" *(Genesis 22:7)*

What did Hazrat Ibrahim say in response to his son? Answer: "Allah himself will provide the lamb for the burnt offering, my son." *(Genesis22:8)*

POINT 2
The True Meaning of Korbani

Introduction question: "What is the meaning behind the practice of Korbani?"

After he gives his answer, say this: "I have studied the before Kitabs (Kitabs = holy books from God), the Taurat (first five books of the Old Testament) and the Injil (New Testament), and have come to understand the way it was practiced and the true meaning behind the act of Korbani."

Say, "Here's what I learned about Korbani from the Kitabs:"

- The *Korbani* animal was to be pure with no blemishes or defects. It cannot be purchased with corrupt money or from the black market.

- *Korbani* is the symbolic act where the guilt and punishment of the sinner is transferred by the judge to the innocent.

- The three participants in the act of Korbani are the animal, representing innocence, man, representing the guilty sinner deserving punishment, and Allah, the merciful judge.

- Hazrut David (David) said that the best Korbani is one that takes place on the inside of a person. Without feeling sorry for your sins, acceptable Korbani is not possible (Psalms 51:16-17).

- Muslim followers of 'Isa stopped the practice of sacrificing animals.

You can then say: *"From the holy Kitabs, I have learned that the correct way to do Korbani is to lay our hands on the animal and say, 'Allah, I know that I am a sinner and that my punishment is eternal death and separation from you. Allah, please take the blood of this animal as a substitute for my punishment, use this blood to cover and remove the evil inside me and the sins of my family.'"*

Korbani was an act done to please Allah so that he would forgive sin. But the forgiveness of sin did not remove the guilt of sin. No judge will say to a repentant murderer, "I know that you are sorry for your crime and therefore, I forgive you, now go and be free." A fair and righteous judge would say to a repentant murderer, "I know you are sorry for your crime, but no matter how sorry you are, someone is still dead, the crime still exists, and punishment must be made."

In order for man to enter into heaven with Allah, man must be holy and totally free from sin. Holiness and unholiness cannot exist in the same place. No matter how repentant and sorry we feel for our sin, punishment for our crime must be paid in full. The punishment for sin is eternal banishment from the presence of Allah.

Since Allah loves us and wants us to be with him in heaven, he made a plan for our salvation and Allah is the best of planners.

POINT 3
The Plan: 'Isa – Korbani for the Whole World!

Allah sent prophets to reveal his wonderful plan to man. He himself would provide the perfect Korbani that would not only cover our sins with forgiveness, but would TOTALLY AND COMPLETELY remove our sins. With sins removed, man can now enter into heaven. The plan itself would reveal to man how much Allah loves him.

The sacrifice had to pure, holy, and powerful enough to cover and remove the sins of all mankind. A sacrifice like this could only come from Allah himself. After reading Surah Al-Imran 3:42-55, you have seen that 'Isa was more than a prophet, that he came directly from Allah, lived a holy life, and had all power in his hand.

Allah decided to demonstrate his love for man by using 'Isa for the sacrifice. The sins of all mankind were placed onto 'Isa. 'Isa took on the entire sins of the world when he died. He did not have to die, but he willingly allowed himself to become the sacrifice for man. The penalty for our crime of sin was paid with the innocent blood of 'Isa.

The Koran says this about 'Isa in Surah Maryam 19:33:

> Peace be on me the day I was born,
> and the day I die,
> and the day I shall be raised alive.

After 'Isa died, the Muslims who followed him stopped doing animal Korbani. They knew that Allah had done the ultimate and complete Korbani. Do you want to have your sins totally and completely removed from you?

POINT 4
Receiving Allah's Gift:
Eternal Life through Believing in 'Isa

A gift is not a gift if you must work for it. When someone gives you a gift, all you have to do to receive the gift is to simply *accept it.*

In the same way, in order to receive Allah's gift of heaven, all you have to do is to accept it. One can try to do enough good works to get into heaven, but in the end, these good works are not enough to remove sins.

The Injil is clear on how to receive Allah's gift. First, understand and know that all men are sinners. Sinners cannot go to heaven and must receive Allah's just punishment of eternity in hell (Romans 3:10-12 and 3;23).

Second, 'Isa was born without sin and never sinned. He is the very "Ruhullah" (Spirit of Allah) and "Kalimatullah" (Word of Allah). His blood is innocent because he did not inherit Adam's sin or commit any sin while alive. 'Isa's blood is holy and powerful ('Isa raised people from the dead). Allah asked Ibrahim to demonstrate his love for Allah by sacrificing his precious son. In the same way, to demonstrate his love for man, Allah decided to do Korbani for all of mankind by sacrificing 'Isa.

Third, 'Isa knew of Allah's plan to use him for the Korbani of the world. Muslim followers of 'Isa are eternally grateful to 'Isa for willingly giving himself to be used for Allah's Korbani. Allah placed the sins of all mankind on 'Isa and then he was killed.

In the Injil in I Peter, Surah 3 ayat 18 we read this: " For 'Isa also suffered once for sins, the just ('Isa) for the unjust (man), that He might bring us to Allah." *And it states, "Greater love has no one than this, than to lay down one's life for his friends."* Yahyah (John) Surah 15, ayat 13.

Fourth, the Injil states that in order to receive Allah's gift of eternal life, a person must believe in 'Isa. In the Injil in Yahyah (John), Surah 3, ayat 16, it says, *"For Allah so loved the world that He gave 'Isa, His Son, that whoever believes in Him should not perish (in hell) but have everlasting life (in heaven)."* It is through 'Isa that we can make it to heaven and live eternally with Allah. 'Isa knows the way and is the way to heaven. If you believe that Allah did Korbani by using the blood of 'Isa to cover and remove your sins, then you can join 'Isa in heaven.

Lift your hands to Allah and say these words:

"Allah, I believe that you are one. I believe that you love all people. I understand that I am a sinner and that I deserve to be forever separated from you when I die. I thank you that you demonstrated your love and mercy for me by doing Korbani for me. I believe that you used 'Isa's blood as the substitute for my blood and punishment. It is through 'Isa that I can now come to you when I die."

After completing the Korbani Plan of Salvation, share the following seven stories from the Bible. Unlike the Korbani Plan of Salvation, the Seven Prophets are to be used with Bible in hand. This study is entitled, "Seven Prophets." Remember that Muslims view all of the major characters of the Bible as prophets.

Seven Prophets

1. Adam (Genesis 2:1-3:24)

Important points:
- Adam was in perfect relationship with God in the Garden.

He saw God, talked with God and knew what God was like.

- God commanded Adam not to eat of the fruit of the Tree of the Knowledge of Good and Evil. God told him that in the day that he ate from it he would die.

- Satan tempted Eve (Muslim name is Hawah) and she ate of the forbidden fruit and she offered it to Adam and he ate of it also. Immediately they felt shame, tried to cover their nakedness and hid from God.

- Adam and Eve did not die physically that day. However they were cast out of the Garden and separated from God that day. In **Romans 3:23,** the Injil tells us that the penalty of sin is death. Death means separation from God who is our life. Physical death entered the world because of sin, but the primary penalty of sin is that it separates us from God.

- Adam and Eve's attempt to cover their shame was useless. But God killed an animal and covered them in animal skin.

Summary: Sin produces death. Death means separation from God who is our life.

2. Abel Genesis chapters 1-16

Important points:

- Cain and Abel brought offerings/sacrifices before the Lord. Cain was a farmer so he brought produce from his fields. Abel was a shepherd so he brought an animal sacrifice.

- God was pleased with Abel's sacrifice which was a blood sacrifice. He was not pleased with Cain's bloodless offering. God showed that he required a blood sacrifice.

- Rather than learn from this experience what kind of offering God required, Cain became jealous and killed his brother.

- Cain's sin and rebellion caused him to be driven even further from the presence of the Lord.

Summary: The blood sacrifice that Abel brought established the requirement of a blood sacrifice until the coming of Jesus (See Hebrews 12:24). Sin brings death which is separation from God.

3. Noah Genesis chapters 6-8

Important points:

- Once man was separated from the presence of God, Satan began to flood the earth with false ideas about who God is and what he requires of man. (See John 8:44 and Revelation 12:9.) The wickedness of man became so great that God decided to destroy mankind from off the earth.

- God chose to spare Noah and his family because Noah was a just man.

- God told Noah to build an ark (a huge box that would float) because he was going to destroy the inhabitants of earth by a flood.

- Noah obeyed God and built the ark.

- When God flooded the earth, Noah and his family were lifted by the ark above the watery judgment of God against wicked and unbelieving mankind.

Summary: Sin brings judgment and death. Those who believe God and apply his appointed means of deliverance will be saved from God's judgment upon sin.

4. Abraham Genesis chapters 12-25

Important points:
- To counter the false ideas about God that Satan had flooded the world with, God chose to raise up a people through whom he would reveal what he is like and what he requires of man.

- As the father of His people, God chose Abraham.

- God told Abraham that he would give him multitudes of physical descendants and through his descendants; God would bless all the families of the earth. So Abraham believed God and followed Him to the land of Canaan.

- Abraham and his wife Sarah had gotten very old (physically too old to have a child) and they still had no child through whom God could give Abraham many descendants. But one night, God took Abraham outside and showed him the stars in the sky and told him that the number of his descendants would be like the stars. Abraham believed God and it was counted unto him for righteousness.

- When Abraham was 100 years old, God gave him a son named Isaac. This was the son that God had promised.

- Later, God commanded Abraham to go and offer Isaac as a sacrifice to God. Abraham obeyed God, but before he could put the knife to Isaac the Angel of the Lord stopped him. Instead of Isaac, God provided a ram for the sacrifice.

Summary: God wants us to know what he is like and what he requires of us. In Abraham we see that right standing before God requires faith. (See Romans 4:1-5.) Also we see that God would not allow Abraham to offer his son as a sacrifice. God provided a substitute. But one day God would offer his Son who would be the substitute for all people of faith. (See John 3:16.)

5. Moses Exodus chapters 12-20

Important points:

- God's people were sent to Egypt. They were treated kindly there at first, but later they were made to be slaves and were treated harshly.

- God raised up Moses to deliver his people from their bondage in Egypt.

- At Moses' command, nine terrible plagues came on Egypt, but Pharaoh would not let God's people go.

- God sent one final plague on Egypt – the first born of every creature was to die. God told his people that they were to sacrifice a lamb and splatter its blood on the doorposts of their houses. God would pass over the houses of those who believed him and applied the lamb's blood and the firstborn there would not die, but live.

- Through this last plague God delivered his people and caused them to pass from Egypt, through the Red Sea and into the wilderness.

- God took His people to Mount Sinai and there he gave them his Law. The purpose of his Law was to reveal his righteousness and what he required of mankind.

- Immediately after God gave Moses his commandments, he told Moses to build an altar so that when the people sinned they might bring a blood sacrifice as an offering for sin.

- For the next 1500 years, until Jesus came, every day the people of Israel saw the penalty of sin – death!

- Those who would be in right standing before God had to bring the offering that God required for their sin.

Summary: In the very fabric of the existence of his people, Israel, God wove the picture of the blood sacrifice. The Passover feast that celebrated their deliverance from bondage reminded them of the lamb that died and became the substitute for them. The constant sacrifices for sin reminded them of the penalty of sin which was death and the animals which became the substitute for them. Those who would be in right standing before God and have their sins forgiven had to offer the proper sacrifice.

6. David I Samuel 16-17 and II Samuel 5-7

Important points:
- God chose David to be king of his people Israel, because David was a man after God's own heart.

- God enabled David to defeat Goliath and to do many other mighty feats to lift David up in the eyes of the people.

- God told David that his throne (rule, authority) would be an everlasting throne. (II Samuel 7:12-13 and Psalms 89:3-4)

Summary: The Messiah or Deliverer that was to come to God's people would be a descendant of David. He would be the King of kings and the Lord of lords.

7. Jesus Matthew, Mark, Luke and John

Important points:
- John the Baptist came to God's people telling them the Messiah that God had promised was coming and the Kingdom of God was at hand.

- When Jesus came to John to be baptized, John looked at him and said, *"Behold! The Lamb of God who takes away the sin of the world!"* (John 1:29) Remember that God's people had a picture burned in their minds which is this: sin produces death, which is separation from God; God provides a substitute which is a blood sacrifice; those who believe God and offer the proper offering are restored to right standing before God. So when John said, the Lamb of God, they knew he meant a sacrifice. But this one, John proclaimed, could take away the sin of the whole world!

- Jesus taught the people the truth of God. In Matthew chapter five he taught us that sin is not just our outward actions, but also the thoughts and intents of our hearts. Just as God told Samuel when he looked at David: "The Lord looks at the heart."

- Jesus lived a sinless life (Hebrews 4:15) Therefore he did not owe the penalty of sin (Romans 6:23) that every descendant of Adam owes.

- Jesus said that he came to pay the penalty of sin. He said, *"For even the Son of Man did not come to be served, but to serve, and to give His life a ransom for many."* (Mark 10:45)

- When Jesus died on the cross, he was not dying to pay for his sin, but for our sin. Right before he died, he said, "It is finished." (John 19:30) In the original language of the New Testament this phrase translated "it is finished" was one word. It was written on a bill when the final payment was made. It meant literally "paid in full". Jesus was saying that as he died our sin debt was paid in full.

- God confirmed that Jesus had indeed paid our penalty for sin by raising him from the dead. (See Romans 1:4 and Acts 17:31.)

Summary: Jesus came to be the sacrifice for our sins. Jesus told us that he was going to die for our sins. Then he died for us and God confirmed that he had accepted the sacrifice of Jesus for the penalty of sin by raising him from the dead.

At this point you should be ready to confront your Muslim friend with his need to receive Jesus as Savior. Here are some verses you can use with him:

And he (Jesus) said to them, "And He said to them, 'Go into all the world and preach the gospel to every creature. [1]He who believes and is baptized will be saved; but he who does not believe will be condemned.'" (Mark 16:15-16)

"But as many as received Him, to them He gave the right to become children of God, to those who believe in His name...." (John 1:12)

"For God so loved the world that He gave His only begotten Son, that whoever believes in Him should not perish but have everlasting life." (John 3:16)

"that if you confess with your mouth the Lord Jesus and believe in your heart that God has raised Him from the dead, you will be saved." (Romans 10:9)

Discipleship Studies

By Randy Owens

Section One:

Introduction

The Korbani plan of salvation may lead a Muslim *Person of Peace* into the family of God, but what comes next? How do you disciple a Muslim-background believer?

The following discipleship studies by Randy Owens were written for new Muslim-background believers. They address worldview issues that are important to new believers emerging from a Muslim environment.

All scripture references are taken from the NKJV.

Your New Life in 'Isa
"10 Studies of Basic Discipleship Principles"

Introduction - How to use these lessons.
In each of these ten lessons:

1. Tell the Injil Story.

2. Discuss the difference between the old life in Islam and the new life in 'Isa.

3. Read or quote the Scriptures and discuss them.

4. Ask these questions at the end of each study:

   • What truth is 'Isa teaching me?
   • How does that truth change my life?
   • What must I do in response to this truth?

5. Begin to learn the memory Scripture.

Be sure to begin each lesson by praying and asking the Holy Spirit to guide you into the truth. Also be sure to end each lesson with a time of prayer and giving praise and thanks to God for what he has done in the lives of each of those involved in the lessons.

Central Theme:
II Corinthians 5:17 If anyone is in Christ, he is a new creation; old things have passed away; behold all things have become new.

1. A New Confession

Injil Story: Paul Believes in 'Isa - Acts 9:1-11
> Saul, a chief Imam among the Jews, rejected the resurrection of 'Isa and severely persecuted those who followed 'Isa. On his way to Damascus to arrest 'Isa's followers, 'Isa appeared to Saul. Saul asked him, "Who are you, **Lord**?" 'Isa answered, "I am 'Isa, whom you persecute." Saul said, "What would you have me to do Lord?" 'Isa told him to go into Damascus where he would be told what to do. There, 'Isa sent a man named Ananias to Saul. Ananias baptized Saul in the name of 'Isa. Saul, who later became known as Paul, began to preach the resurrection of 'Isa and the forgiveness of sin and eternal life through faith in 'Isa. People were amazed that this Saul, who had persecuted those who followed 'Isa, was now calling them to confess 'Isa as Lord and follow him!

> God later used Paul to start many jamats and write a large part of the Injil. Who knows how God might choose to use you?

Old confession

"There is no God but God and Mohammed is his prophet."

New Confession
"Jesus is Lord."

John 17:3 ('Isa) "This is eternal life to know you the only true God and Jesus Christ whom you have sent."

Acts 2:36-38 God has made this Jesus whom you crucified both Lord and Christ (Masi). And when they heard this they were cut to the heart and they said ... "What shall we do?" Then Peter said unto them, "Repent, and let everyone of you be baptized in the Name of Jesus Christ and you shall receive the gift of the Holy Spirit."

Romans 10:9 If you confess with your mouth the Lord Jesus and believe in your heart that God has raised Him from the dead you shall be saved.

Acts 4:10-12 'Isa Masi ... Neither is there any other name under heaven given unto men whereby we must be saved.

John 14:6 Jesus said to him, "I am the way the truth and the life. No one comes to the father except through me."

QUESTIONS:

MEMORY SECTION
Romans 10:9-10, 13 If you confess with your mouth the Lord Jesus and believe in your heart that Allah has raised him from the dead, you shall be saved. For with the heart one believes unto righteousness, and with the mouth confession is made unto salvation. For whosoever calls upon the Name of the Lord shall be saved.

2. A New and Certain Hope of Eternal Life
Injil Story: The Good Shepherd – John 10:1-30

'Isa compares his love and care for us to that of a good shepherd. Sheep come to know the voice of their shepherd and they will not follow a strange voice. Their shepherd feeds them, cares for them and protects them from their enemies. A good shepherd will lay down his life to protect his sheep. Jesus laid down his life for us so that we could be forgiven of our sins and have eternal life. Now our good shepherd, 'Isa, nurtures and leads us so that we can experience abundant life through Him. We must learn to hear his voice, for, according to John 10:10, all the other voices are those of thieves and robbers. They only want to kill by eternal death and separation from God, and steal and destroy the abundant life he wants us to experience in 'Isa.

Note: Two possible stories are included here. You can use one or both of them to help establish this important truth of the assurance of salvation.

Injil Story: The Dying Criminal – Luke 23:32-43

When 'Isa was put to death on the cross (crucified) two criminals were crucified with him; one on either side. One mocked and ridiculed 'Isa, saying, "if you are the Christ/Masi save yourself and us!" However, the other criminal rebuked the first criminal. He admitted that he deserved to be there dying for his crimes, but that 'Isa had done nothing wrong. Then he looked to 'Isa for mercy and asked him to remember him when he entered into his kingdom. 'Isa said to him, "Today you shall be with Me in paradise." The criminal received a promise of eternal life in paradise/heaven with 'Isa. These three crosses represent all of humanity. Through 'Isa, God entered the human race to deliver humanity from the condemnation of sin and the power of the devil. Many, like the first criminal, reject Jesus and die in their sin, eternally separated from God. But those who are like the second criminal and ask for mercy and forgiveness in 'Isa's name will be given eternal life in 'Isa.

Old Hope of Paradise/Heaven

Observe the five pillars of Islam. Do good works. Maybe God might accept you into paradise, but one cannot know. Only if God wills!

New Hope of Paradise/Heaven

'Isa has died to pay the penalty of your sin. You are forgiven and made right before God. By faith in 'Isa you have sure hope of eternal life in heaven.

I Peter 3:18 Christ/Masi has suffered, once, the righteous for the unrighteous that he might bring us to God.

John 6:47 Most assuredly, I say to you, he that believes in me ('Isa) has everlasting life.

John 10:27-30 My sheep hear My voice and I know them and they follow Me and I give them eternal life, and they shall never perish, neither shall anyone snatch them out of My hand. My Father, Who gave them to Me is greater than all; and no one can snatch them out of His hands. I and My Father are one.

Romans 8:38-39 For I am persuaded that neither death nor life, nor principalities nor powers, nor things present nor things to come, nor height nor depth, nor nay other created thing, shall be able to separate us from the love of God which is in 'Isa Masi our Lord.

QUESTIONS:

MEMORY SECTION
John 10:27-28 My sheep hear My voice and I know them and they follow Me and I give them eternal life and they shall never perish, neither shall anyone snatch them out of My hand.

3. A New Family

Injil Story: The First Jamat – Acts 2:38-42

In this section of the Injil we get to see the very first Jamat of 'Isa and what it was like. We find it was like a family who loved one another and cared for the needs of one another. They frequently gathered together to study the teachings of 'Isa that had been preserved for them by the apostles of 'Isa (which we have in the Injil). They also had fellowship with one another and prayed together. They took the bread and juice of the Lord's Supper to remember what 'Isa had done for them in His death on the cross. They were filled with joy and praised God together. They were obeying the command of 'Isa to love God and love one another.

Old Family
The family you were born into.

New Family
The family of God through the Jamat of 'Isa.

Note: This does not mean you forsake the family you were born into, but rather that now you have the expanded blessings of being part of God's family in the world and having all the other followers of 'Isa as brothers and sisters in 'Isa. Sadly, friends and family may sometimes forsake the new follower of 'Isa, but God gives you a wonderful promise in His word: "When my father and mother forsake me, then the Lord will take care of me." **Psalm 27:10**

Ephesians 3:14 I bow my knees to the Father of our Lord 'Isa Masi from whom the whole family in heaven and on earth is named.

John 15:12 This is my ('Isa's) commandment that you love one another as I have loved you.

Hebrews 13:1 Let brotherly love continue.

Galatians 6:10 Therefore, as we have opportunity let us do good to all, especially to those who are of the household of faith.

Ephesians 4:32 Be kind to one another, tender-hearted, forgiving one another just as God for 'Isa Masi's sake has forgiven you.

QUESTIONS:

MEMORY SECTION

John 13:34-35 A new commandment I give you, that you love one another as I have loved you. By this all will know that you are My disciples, if you have love for one another.

4. A New Way to Pray

Injil Story: Teach Us To Pray - Matthew 6:5-14

The disciples of Jesus often watched 'Isa as he prayed. They asked him to teach them to pray (Luke 11:1). This section of the Injil (in Matthew) tells us the way 'Isa taught them and us to pray. He told us that we should not be like the outwardly religious people who pray so that others would see them, but rather that we should go into a secret place and pray to our Father in heaven. He also taught us not to repeat empty memorized words and phrases, but to pray from the heart like a child speaking to his Father and asking something of him. He said we don't have to beg and plead with the Father, because He knows what we need even before we ask. Then he taught his disciples a prayer. This, of course, is not a prayer to be repeated for 'Isa had just said not to use empty repetition. It is instead a pattern of how we should pray. Finally, he reminded us that if we will pray to God to ask his supply, forgiveness and help, we must be willing to forgive those who have harmed us.

Old Way To Pray

Pray five times daily, repeating memorized prayer. Answers were seldom or never seen.

New Way to Pray

Talk to God as a child speaks to his father, asking Him to work in your life and expecting Him to answer.

Because 'Isa has removed our sin by his blood we now have bold access to the very presence of God - **Ephesians 3:12** 'Isa Masi our Lord, in whom we have boldness and access with confidence through faith in him.

Matthew 7:7-11 Ask and it will be given to you; seek and you shall find; knock and the door shall be opened unto you. For everyone who asks receives, and he who seeks finds, and to him who knocks it will be opened. Or what man is there among you, if his son asks him for bread, will give him a stone? Or if he asks for a fish will he give him a snake? If you then, being evil, know how to give good gifts to your children, how much more will your Father Who is in heaven give good things to those who ask Him!

John 14:12-14 Most assuredly I say to you, he that believes in Me, the works that I do shall he do also, and greater works shall he do because I go to the Father. And whatever you ask in my name, that will I do that the Father may be glorified in the Son. If you shall ask anything in my name, I will do it.

Philippians 4:6-7 Don't worry about anything, but in everything by prayer and supplication with thanksgiving let your requests be made known to God and the peace of God which passes knowledge will guard your hearts and minds through 'Isa Masi.

I Thessalonians 5:17 Pray without ceasing.

Hebrews 4:16 Let us therefore come boldly to the throne of grace, that we may obtain mercy and find grace and help in time of need.

QUESTIONS:

MEMORY SECTION

John 16:24 Until now you have asked nothing in my ('Isa) name. Ask and receive that your joy may be full.

5. A New Access to Truth

Injil Story: The Vine and the Branches - John 15:1-8
'Isa compared the relationship we have with him to the connection of a vine (or tree) and its branches. Through 'Isa we are connected to the very life of God. His life flowing through us produces the fruit of 'Isa in our lives. Just as the branch cannot bear fruit without the vine, or tree, even so we cannot bear eternal fruit apart from 'Isa. 'Isa tells us how this relationship works. He said, "if you abide in me and My Words abide in you, you shall ask what you desire and it shall be done unto you, for by this is my Father glorified that you bear much fruit." The follower of 'Isa needs to fill his mind and heart with the truth of the Injil. The words of 'Isa abide in us through a process the Bible calls "meditation". It simply means "to repeat over and over again" or "to ponder". Meditation upon the words of 'Isa is very simple. Over time it will have a great impact upon your life. Meditation involves 4 simple steps. <u>First</u> you must hear a section of the Injil; <u>then</u> you must memorize it; <u>then</u> you must ponder it (think upon it) over and over until 'Isa gives you understanding; <u>then</u> you must do what it says. By this process of abiding in 'Isa through prayer, and his words abiding in you through meditation, you will become a "true branch" through which 'Isa produces eternal fruit.

The Old Access to Truth
Memorize the Koran and repeat words without understanding them.

The New Access to Truth
Read and understand the Taurat, Zabur, Nobis (Prophets) and the Injil. Meditate upon the truths you learn and obey them and see eternal fruit produced in your life.

Psalm 1:1-2 Blessed is the man who walks not in the counsel of the ungodly, nor stands in the path of sinners, nor sits in the seat of the scornful; but his delight is in the Law of the Lord, and in His Law he meditates day and night. He shall be like a tree planted by the rivers of water, that brings forth its fruit in season, whose leaf does not wither, and whatsoever he does shall prosper.

John 8:31-32 And 'Isa said, "If you abide in My word you are My disciples indeed, and you shall know the truth and the truth shall make you free.

Philippians 4:8 Brethren, whatever things are true ... meditate on these things. The things you learned and received and heard and saw in me do, and the very God of peace will be with you.

I Timothy 4:13-15 Give attention to reading, encouragement and doctrine (Injil teachings)... meditate on these things and give yourself entirely to them that your progress may be evident to all.

QUESTIONS:

MEMORY SECTION
John 15:7-8 If you abide in Me and My words abide in you, you will ask what you desire and it shall be done to you. By this is my Father glorified, that you bear much fruit; so shall you be my disciples.

6. A New Freedom

Injil Story: Stand Firm in Your Freedom
Galatians 2:16-21, 5:1-14, Philippians 3:3

Paul, the apostle of 'Isa, had gone into a region called Galatia, preached the good news of eternal life in 'Isa and as a result several jamats had been started there. He had clearly taught them that salvation and eternal life came through simple faith in 'Isa, their Korbani (sacrifice) for sin' and not in religious works. Later some false teachers had come to the churches and told them that if they wanted to go to heaven, they needed to add to their faith in 'Isa a strict observance of the Jewish laws. Paul wrote in them a letter to teach the truth. It is the letter to the Galatians in the Injil. He told them that their faith and hope of eternal life rested upon the fact that 'Isa had died for their sins. The righteous anger of God against sin had been satisfied in 'Isa's sacrifice and their salvation was the gift of his grace. He said, "I do not set aside the grace of God, for if righteousness comes by the law then Christ/Masi died in vain (for nothing)." Paul told them not to become entangled again in a yoke of bondage of religious works, or even good works, to try to earn God's favor. God's favor rests on those who trust in 'Isa. We have been saved and set free from the penalty of sin and the bondage of works. He warned them to be careful, however, not to use their freedom as an opportunity to indulge the flesh, such as sexual immorality, drunkenness, greed and such things, but rather to use their freedom to serve 'Isa and to love one another.

Old Bondage

Strictly observe the five pillars of Islam, try to do good and hope that somehow it will be enough and God will be pleased with you.

New Freedom

Trust in 'Isa and put no hope at all in your good works, knowing that he will give you eternal life in heaven. You are free! Rejoice in your freedom in 'Isa and use it to serve him and to love your brothers and sisters in 'Isa.

Philippians 3:3 For we are the circumcision (true followers of God) who worship God in the Spirit, rejoice in 'Isa Masi, and have no confidence in the flesh.

Philippians 4:4 Rejoice in the Lord always and again I say rejoice.

I Peter 2:15-16 For this is the will of God, that by doing good you may put to silence the ignorance of foolish men as free men, not using liberty as a cloak for vice (cover for doing wrong), but as bondservants of God.

QUESTIONS:

MEMORY SECTION
Galatians 5:1, 13 Stand fast therefore in the liberty by which Christ/Masi has made us free and do not be entangled again in a yoke of bondage. For you, brethren have been called to liberty; only do not use liberty as an opportunity for the flesh, but through love serve one another.

7. A New Relationship to God

Injil Story: A Rushing Mighty Wind – Acts 2:1-41

The night before 'Isa was crucified he told his disciples, "I will pray to the Father and He will give you another Comforter – the Spirit of Truth. I will not leave you as orphans, I will come to you. At that day you will know that I am in the Father and you are in me and I am in you." (John 14:16-20) When the Roman soldiers took Jesus to crucify him, the disciples of 'Isa ran and hid. While he was buried in the tomb they hid in fear. After 'Isa rose from the dead, he appeared to his disciples and reminded them that when he ascended back to the Father in heaven that He would send another Helper to live in them – the Holy Spirit of God. To his fearful disciples he said, "You shall receive power after the Holy Spirit has come upon you and you shall be witnesses to me... to the end of the earth." Then the Holy Spirit came upon them like a "mighty rushing wind." They were never the same after that. They suddenly became bold and fearless witnesses of 'Isa, and spread the gospel of 'Isa throughout the world.

Old Relationship

Alone and only understanding God as a distant presence, unknowable to men.

New Relationship

'Isa dwelling in you through the Holy Spirit of God. He is your Comforter, Friend, and Helper as you serve him each day.

Acts 2:38 Repent and let every one of you be baptized in the name of 'Isa Masi for the forgiveness of sins and you shall receive the gift of the Holy Spirit.

Ephesians 1:13-14 In him ('Isa) you also trusted after you heard the word of truth, the gospel of your salvation; in whom also having believed, you were sealed with the promised Holy Spirit.

John 16:7 It is to your advantage that I ('Isa) go away, for if I do not go away, the Helper will not come to you, but if I depart, I will send Him to you ... When He, the Spirit of Truth has come, He will guide you into all truth.

Hebrews 13:5 I will never leave you nor forsake you.

Proverbs 18:24 There is a friend that sticks closer than a brother.

QUESTIONS:

MEMORY SECTION

I Corinthians 3:16 Do you not know that you are the temple of God and that the Spirit of God dwells in you?

8. A New Purpose in Life

Injil Story: Fishing for Men - **Luke 5:1-11**

Peter was a fisherman. One day 'Isa came where Peter fished, got into his boat and asked Peter if he would put his boat out a little way from the shore so that 'Isa could teach the crowds that pressed around him. After he had finished teaching the people, 'Isa asked Peter to launch his boat out into the deep water and drop his nets to catch fish. Peter told Jesus he had been fishing all night and had caught nothing. But because 'Isa asked him, Peter and his partners went back out fishing. When they let down their nets, they caught so many fish that their nets were breaking and their boats were about to sink. When they got back to shore Peter fell down at 'Isa's feet and said, "Depart from me for I am a sinful man, O Lord!" 'Isa told Peter, "Do not be afraid; From now on you will catch men." At 'Isa's call, Peter left all he had and followed 'Isa. Peter's life was never the same! After 'Isa was raised from the dead and ascended in heaven, Peter was used powerfully by God to proclaim the good news of salvation in 'Isa and bring many to salvation in 'Isa. Peter's life made an incredible eternal impact on this world!

Old Purpose in Life
You were taught to try to do enough good works to go to heaven and then hope you would make it. Do your best to survive each day.

New Purpose in Life
You are called to worship God, grow as a disciple of 'Isa and make new disciples (Be a fisher of men).

Matthew 28:18-20 All authority has been given to Me in heaven and on the earth. Go therefore and make disciples of all nations, baptizing them in the name of the Father, the Son and the Holy Spirit, teaching them to observe all things that I have commanded you; and lo I am with you always, even to the end of the age.

Colossians 3:23-24 And whatever you do, do it heartily as to the Lord and not to men, knowing that from the Lord you will receive the reward of the inheritance; for you serve the Lord Christ/Masi.

I Corinthians 15:1-4 Brothers, I declare unto you the gospel ("good news") which I preached to you, which also you received and in which you stand, by which also you are saved, if you hold fast that word which I preached to you – unless you believed in vain. For I delivered unto you first of all that which I also received, that Christ/Masi died for our sins according to the Scriptures and that He was buried, and that He rose again on the third day, according to the Scriptures.

QUESTIONS:

MEMORY SECTION

II Corinthians 5:21 Now we are ambassadors for Christ/Masi as though God were pleading through us on 'Isa's behalf to be reconciled to God. For he made him ('Isa) who knew no sin to be sin for us, that we might become the righteousness of God in him.

9. A New Hope of Reward

Injil Story: The Faithful Servants – Luke 19:11-27
> 'Isa told this story to show us what we can expect when the Day of Judgment comes. Read these two verses and then tell the story.

Acts 17:31 Because he (God) has appointed a day on which he will judge the world in righteousness by the man whom he has ordained. He has given assurance of this to all by raising him from the dead.

II Corinthians 5:10 For we must all appear before the judgment seat of Christ/Masi, that each one may receive the things done in the body, according to what he has done, whether good or bad.

> A wealthy man traveled to a far country. He called in his servants and distributed his goods to them and told them to do his business while he was gone. He gave to some more than others, just as we all have different levels of wealth, abilities and opportunities. When he returned, he called his servants in to give an account. Those who faithfully

sought to do his business received great rewards. The master did not rebuke the servant with five talents for not making ten. 'Isa holds you accountable only for what he has given you, not what he has given another. Each faithful servant of 'Isa can look forward to hearing these blessed words, "Well done, good and faithful servant; you have been faithful over a few things, I will make you ruler over many things. Enter the joy of you Lord!"

Old Hope of Reward

Will I even enter paradise? Will there be any eternal rewards for me?

New Hope of Reward

'Isa has already secured for me my entry into heaven/paradise. Now by His Spirit He will enable me to serve him and then he will eternally reward my faithful service to him.

Ephesians 2:4-7 But God ... has made us alive together with Christ/Masi ... that in the ages to come He might show the exceeding riches of His grace in His kindness toward us in 'Isa.

Matthew 5:11 Blessed are you when they revile and persecute you, and say all kinds of evil against you falsely for my ('Isa's) sake. Rejoice and be exceedingly glad, for great is your reward in heaven.

Revelation 22:12 Behold, I ('Isa) am coming quickly, and my reward is with me to give to everyone according to his work.

QUESTIONS:

MEMORY SECTION

Matthew 25:23 Well done, good and faithful servant; you have been faithful over a few things, I will make you ruler over many things. Enter into the joy of you Lord.

10. A New Resistance

Injil Story: Counting the Costs – Luke 14:25-33

Because he healed the sick, taught with authority and spoke of eternal life and rewards, great crowds followed 'Isa everywhere he went. But 'Isa did not deceive anyone about the cost of following Him. One day he stopped, turned to the crowd and said, "if anyone comes to Me and does not hate his father and mother, wife and children, brother and sister, yes and his own life also, he cannot be my disciple." What an astounding statement! Of course he did not literally mean we were to hate our family. The Injil itself commands you to honor your father and mother and love your wife like 'Isa has loved us. What 'Isa meant was that we must love him supremely. If we have to choose between family and 'Isa we must choose 'Isa. To come and follow 'Isa is to choose him above all else. The cost of following 'Isa is often very high. Consider these Scriptures:

John 15:19-20 If you were of the world the world would love its own. Yet because you are not of the world, but I ('Isa) chose you out of the world, therefore the world hates you. Remember the word that I said to you, "A servant is not greater than his master." If they persecuted me they will persecute you also. If they have kept my word, they will keep yours also.

II Timothy 3:12 Yes, and all who desire to live godly in 'Isa Masi will suffer persecution.

Old Resistance
There was little or no resistance. An old proverb says, "Let sleeping dogs lie." Before you came to 'Isa and began to tell of the good news of eternal life in 'Isa, the devil left you alone for you caused his kingdom no harm.

New Resistance
Because you now belong to 'Isa and seek to tells others about a Him, the devil attacks you through those that belong to him.

'Isa told the crowd that followed him that they should consider the costs of following him. One would not begin to build a house if he knew he did not have enough money to finish it. Neither should we follow after 'Isa, unless we are willing to accept the cost. This is very hard to hear, but listen to the good news of the verses that follow:

Romans 8:16-18 The Spirit himself bears witness with our spirit that we are indeed the children of God, and if children, heirs – heirs of God and joint heirs with 'Isa, if indeed we suffer with him that we may also be glorified with Him. For I consider the sufferings of this present time not worthy to be compared with the glory that will be revealed in us.

II Corinthians 4:17 For our light affliction which is but for a moment, is producing for us a far more exceeding and eternal weight of glory, while we look not on the things that are seen but the things that are unseen. For the things that are seen are temporary, but the things that are unseen are eternal.

Luke 18:29-30 He ('Isa) said to them, "Assuredly I say to you, there is no one who has left house or parents or brothers or wife or children, for the sake of the kingdom of God who shall not receive many times more in this present age and in the age to come eternal life."

QUESTIONS:

MEMORY SECTION

Matthew 5:11 Blessed are you when they revile and persecute you and say all kinds of evil against you falsely for my sake. Rejoice and be exceedingly glad, for great is your reward in heaven, for so they persecuted the prophets that were before you.

Section Two:

What kind of new church would you like to see? The first church in Acts is a good model. To pattern your church after the first church in the Bible, lead your group through these studies from the book of Acts.

Discipleship Studies from the Book of ACTS

Seven Questions to ask about each story:

1. What did God do?

2. How did the followers of 'Isa respond?

3. How did those who were not followers of 'Isa respond?

4. Was the Jamat (Church) of 'Isa helped or hurt?

5. What do you like about this story?

6. What troubles you about this story?

7. Through this story, what is God telling you to do?

Stories from the Book of Acts

1. ACTS 1:1-11

Jesus appears to His followers and tells them to wait for the Holy Spirit to come and empower them to be His witnesses. Then He ascends into heaven.

2. ACTS 2:1-41

The Holy Spirit comes upon the disciples and they preach with power and in languages they do not know. Peter preaches and 3000 people are saved and baptized in one day.

3. ACTS 2:41-47

The first Jamat is formed and we see what it is like.

4. ACTS 3

A lame man is healed and Peter uses the opportunity to tell the good news of the forgiveness of sins and eternal life in Jesus.

5. ACTS 4

The religious leaders in Jerusalem begin to stand up against the preaching of the good news of Jesus.

6. ACTS 5:1-16

Jesus purifies his Jamat of the sin of hypocrisy (pretending to be what you are not in order to receive the honor of men).

7. ACTS 5:17-42

Persecution (from the religious leaders) begins to rise up against the young Jamat in Jerusalem.

8. ACTS 6:1-7

Having first failed to corrupt the new Jamat (Acts 5:1-6), the devil attempts to sow discord.

9. ACTS 6:8-7:60

Stephen becomes the first martyr (one who is killed directly because of his faith in Jesus) of the Jamat.

10. ACTS 8

Persecution of the followers of 'Isa becomes intense, so many of them begin to go and proclaim the good news of Jesus in other places, just as Jesus had said in Acts 1:8. Phillip leads a non-Israelite to faith in Jesus and baptizes him.

11. ACTS 9

Saul, the chief persecutor of 'Isa Jamats, is confronted by Jesus and comes to faith in him. His name is changed to Paul (Acts 13:9) and he becomes the main agent for taking the good news of 'Isa to the Gentiles (non-Jews).

12. ACTS 10

Peter is commanded by God to take the good news of 'Isa to a Gentile named Cornelius. Cornelius and his household believe in 'Isa and are baptized. The door is thus opened to take the good news of forgiveness of sins and the gift eternal in Jesus into the whole world.

APPENDIX 5

Notes from the Best Church Planters

I have sat beside some of the best evangelists to Muslims as they spoke to Muslims. Below are my notes from what I have heard through the years as these evangelists responded to common arguments from Muslims.

The Koran says that 'Isa did not die

The Koran never says that 'Isa didn't die. Muslims use Surah Al-Nisa 4:157 to say that Jews did not kill 'Isa. This is true because in that period of time, the Jews were not allowed to put anyone to death (John 18:31), only the Romans could do that. Furthermore, the Koran never states that Jesus did not die.

Christians are not Muslims

This issue arises because many Christian evangelists to Muslims prefer to introduce themselves as Muslim or 'Isahi Muslim. Every Muslim knows that the word "Muslim" means "one who surrenders himself totally to God." They also claim that all of the prophets such as Adam, Nuh, Ibrahim, Musa, Daud, 'Isa, Peter, etc... were Muslims. Yet, many become upset when Christian evangelists introduce themselves as Muslims or as Isahi Muslims.

The common response by Christian evangelists is as follows. First, Muslims before the time of Mohammed did not say, "God is one and Mohammed is his prophet" in order to become Muslim. Secondly, the Koran in Surah Al-Imran 3:52 refers to the followers of 'Isa as Muslims. And finally, technically there is only one true Muslim that has ever totally submitted himself to God and that was 'Isa. He is the only true Muslim.

Ishmael versus Isaac debate

Muslims believe that the Koran claims Ishmael was the son who Ibrahim took with him to sacrifice on the mountain. Actually though, the Koran does not say which son. The story of Ibrahim's attempted sacrifice is found in Surah As-Saffat-Ruku 37:100-111. In this passage, the son's name is not mentioned.

If you can get your Muslim friend to read this story in the Koran, don't let them stop at ayat 111. Encourage him to continue reading. As he reads on, he will quickly see the Koran's praise of Isaac. Ask them if they can find Ishmael's name in this Surah. Ishmael is nowhere near this story in the Koran.

In addition, explain to them that the test of love given by God involved the sacrifice of Ibrahim's most precious possession. Ibrahim had two precious sons, but one stands out. It makes sense that the son who came from Sarah, his longstanding wife, and who was born miraculously should be considered as the exceptional son.

The son born from the house maid, whose name means "Wild donkey," and was sent away from the tribe with his mother naturally should be considered the lesser of the two sons. This is a good opportunity to point out the prophecy told about Ishmael and his descendents, "That his hand will be against everyone and that everyone will be against him." (Genesis 16:12) Ask, "What do you think about this prophecy?"

Prophets do not sin... or do they?

Surah Ta Ha 20:121 exposes the sin of the first prophet Adam, "Then they (Adam and his wife) both ate of it, so their evil inclinations became manifest to them, and they both began to cover themselves with leaves of the garden, and Adam disobeyed his Lord, so his life became evil." Surah Al-Fat Ruku 48:2 tells us of another prophet (guess who?) that would receive forgiveness of sins from the past and for sins yet to be committed in the future, "That God may forgive thee thy faults of the past and those to follow...." Only the prophet 'Isa did not ever commit a sin. This causes 'Isa to stand out among the prophets. Could it be that 'Isa was more than a prophet?

"Only the Arabic Koran is acceptable"
When you mention the Koran, you should be aware that many Muslims believe the only true Koran is the Koran that is in Arabic. They believe that any translation of the Koran is a paraphrase or deviation from the original. Some may use this to discount your claim to have read the Koran. Should this happen, you might try the following:

First say, "I want to give special thanks to King Fahd of Saudi Arabia and the Islamic Foundation for translating the Koran into local languages all over the world for clear understanding."

Then offer the following story:

The foreign owner of a garment factory in an Asian country received a new order for shirts, so he wrote a letter in English to his factory workers telling them that they should stop making red shirts. The letter stated, "Beginning Monday, the factory will cease from making red shirts and begin making yellow shirts." If successful in making this transition, each factory worker would receive a bonus at the end of the month. The Asian office manager related to the factory workers on behalf of the American owner because he could speak, read, and write both the local language and English fluently. On Friday, the office manager gathered all of the factory workers in a room for a meeting. He placed the letter on the table in front of the workers. The workers were happy to receive the letter from their factory owner. They were excited and proud that he had written them a letter. Seeing that all the workers were happy, the office manager returned to his office without saying a word. On Monday, the factory continued to make red shirts. At the end of the month, the warehouse was full of red shirts ready to be shipped. When the factory owner came for inspection, he discovered a warehouse full of red shirts. He burned with anger. The office manager was immediately fired. The factory workers, instead of receiving a bonus, received a reduction in their salary.

Conclude by saying, "In order to know what God wants us to do and believe, we must not just hear what he says, we must **understand** what he says!" Most will certainly agree. This story should prepare the way for your Muslim friend to read the Koran in a local or English language translation.

In the Bible, 'Isa said that Mohammed will come after him

Many Muslims will tell you that Mohammed's coming is mentioned by Jesus in the Bible. They do not know where in the Bible this claim is made, but nevertheless they believe it is there because someone influential to them told them it was. This is a good opportunity to get them to re-examine their confidence in their influential Islamic teacher and to get them into the Bible.

Tell them that you know the ayats in the Bible that refer to what he is talking about. If your Muslim friend is willing, direct him to read John chapters 14-16. If it appears that your friend will not read the entire chapters, then sit beside him and ask him to read out loud John 14:16-17, 26, 15:26, and 16:5-14. Then read together all of Acts 2.

Islam is the greatest religion!

If you work among Muslims, you will inevitably hear this statement. The next time you hear this statement, agree with them. Tell them that among all the major religions today, Islam is on top. For those earning their way to heaven, Islam offers the most comprehensible and complete set of rules. Remember that the word "Religion" means "man's attempts to get to God."

You want rules to live by? Islam has it all. It teaches how to dress, wash, clean one's nose, walk on the road, the proper position of prayer, the times for prayer, what to pray for, whom to marry, how to bury, etc.... The second best religion is Judaism. It has ten commandments. Next is Christianity with two rules, "Love God with all your heart and your neighbor as yourself." Hinduism is next, followed by Buddhism.

Getting into heaven by following the rules is an impossible task. Only Christianity has the answer to this problem. Christianity is based on a relationship with God. Christians try to obey God's rules, not to earn a ticket into heaven, but because they have a ticket to heaven. If you think you can earn your way to heaven, just try it. If you realize that you cannot, then look into Christianity.

'Isa, Son of God

Muslims consider this to be a blasphemous statement. They think that you are actually saying that God took on human qualities and had relations with Mary. To them, this is evil.

To help them understand that you are not making such a claim about God, use the following illustration:

Let's say that 'Isa was alive as a young boy in this city and it came time for him to go to school for the first time. Once he arrives at the school, what two questions will the headmaster give 'Isa? First, he will ask 'Isa, "What is your name?" Naturally, 'Isa will say his name. Secondly, the headmaster will ask 'Isa, "What is the name of your father?"

Ask, "What answer would 'Isa give?" If he answers, "'Isa would say, God." Immediately stop them and say, "That's all that I am saying, nothing more than what you just said." I am not saying anything bad about God.

Photocopy, cut, and place in your pocket

CAMEL METHOD

1. **Opening Statement:** *"I have discovered an amazing truth in the Koran that gives hope of eternal life in heaven. Would you read Surah Al-Imran 3:42-55 so we can talk about it?"*

2. **Three points that help raise Jesus ('Isa) up to Savior Status**
   - **'Isa is holy** – 3:42-48
   - **'Isa has power over death** – 3:49-54
   - **'Isa knows the way to heaven** – 3:55

3. **Final Question:** *"I want to go to heaven when I die. Which prophet can help me get there?"*

Secondary outline method for English speakers

Camel Method
Surah Al-Imran 3:42-55

   Chosen – 3:42-44

   Announcement – 3:45-47

   Miracles – 3:49

   Eternal **L**ife 3:55

WIGTake Resources

Orders for **Church Planting Movements** by David Garrison or **Camel Training Manual** by Kevin Greeson are filled by LANForce Book Fulfillment, a division of LANForce Inc.

U.S. Toll free phone: (888) 795-4434 or (806) 795-4434
U.S. Toll free fax orders: (888) 795-4471 or (806) 795-4471
Email: customerservice@inforceinc.com

Or visit us on the web at www.lanforceinc.com

Single copies $18.95 each*
10-49 @ $17.95 each*
50 copies or more @ $15.95 each*
(*plus shipping & handling)

Single copies $ 8.95 each*
50 copies or more @ $ 7.95 each*
(*plus shipping & handling)

cut here

··

Number of copies_____

Mail book(s) to:
Name   _____
Address   _____
City/State   _____
Country & Postal Code _____

Credit Card Information: ___ MasterCard
                           ___ Visa
                           ___ American Express

Name as it appears on the card: _____
Expiration date: _____
Credit Card Number: _____
(Allow 2 weeks for delivery)